PRAISE FOR THE TRISPECTIVE GROUP

"This is a must-read for anyone who wants to know how to actually build a great team. It is centered on the foundation that great teams are about great relationships that are built on trust and candid feedback. The authors showcase their insight by walking through the good and the bad from the thousands of teams they have worked with, sharing concrete, practical steps any leader can use to improve the culture in their workplace. *The Loyalist Team* introduces a new paradigm for leadership that is required to compete in today's business world."

—Rob Katz, CEO, Vail Resorts, Inc.

"The Loyalist Model really took hold here. It is part of the foundation of our culture and values. We have worked with many business consultants, and the Loyalist model stood out as a very effective framework that allowed us to focus on the importance of communal success. We only succeed by helping each other."

—Steve Smith, CEO, Equinix

"With the Loyalist Team Model, I am really clear about what is required of me as a leader and as importantly what is required of the team to build a really successful Loyalist organization. I know I can never take the human dynamics on a team for granted."

—Mike Goodwin, SVP and Chief Information Officer, PetSmart

"Trispective has become much more than an external resource—they have become integral "adjunct" members of our team. An extension of ourselves. Partners we trust that are fully integrated into the organization. This full integration has ensured alignment on approach, values, language, and desired outcomes. Most importantly, their work has made a lasting and positive difference at Vail Resorts."

—Mark Gasta, former Executive Vice President and
   Chief People Officer, Vail Resorts Management Company

"Right now, this team, my team is the best team I have ever led. We're not perfect, but we are working really hard with the support of Trispective to become a Loyalist Team. I know that we are making progress because of the reactions I see when we are under stress. In recent months, as a business, we've faced some really tough challenges. As we address those challenges, it will create significant opportunities for us. We're charting new territory for this team. The stakes are high, and we have to move quickly. The team has come to me and said, 'We've got your back. Let's move forward. We can do this.' It feels great, and we are being successful."

—Enrique Escalante, CEO, Grupo Cementos de Chihuahua

"It helped me enormously to engage with Trispective and the Loyalist Team Model. When I was confronted with a Saboteur, my natural instinct was to fight—but that wasn't getting me anywhere. I really think understanding the model and working with someone who helped me learn how to deal with a Saboteur made all the difference. Using the Loyalist Model, I was able to reframe the situation and move it to a different place, taking into consideration the goals, objectives, and drivers of the Saboteur. I don't know if I would still be here without that."

—Grant Wicklund, CEO, Lutheran Medical Center

"The most challenging aspect of building a high-performing team is to know and understand each other deeply and to trust one another entirely. Using the Loyalist Team Model, Trispective has supported us in working through the layers of each individual team member to understand who we are. Assuming positive intent on the part of others has opened new, powerful levels of engagement for successful joint outcomes."

—Cindy Paulson, Chief Technical Officer, Brown and Caldwell

"The biggest difference between good and great teams is the ability to have the hardest conversations in the room, not outside of the room. Using the Loyalist Team framework, my team has become a great team on the way to becoming a Loyalist Team by having the tough conversations. On great teams, everyone respects not just each other's opinions but each other's values. And the common values of the team make it possible to have the hardest of discussions on the hardest of issues—discussions that only make the team stronger."

—Tom Boasberg, Superintendent, Denver Public Schools

"Some of the toughest lessons I've learned along my leadership journey have come when I've underestimated or undervalued the amount of time I need to spend on my team. The Loyalist Team Model provided a framework and understanding of where to invest in my team. We've been able to get clear about the end goal, through having the uncomfortable conversations, debating the trade-offs, taking the time to really hear each other's perspectives, and ultimately making the changes needed to get there, even when it includes changing the team up. Loyalist Teams don't happen, they are built, with hard work every step of the way."

—Suzanne Sanchez, Chief Human Resources Officer, Great-West Financial

The Loyalist Team

HOW TRUST, CANDOR,
and AUTHENTICITY CREATE
GREAT ORGANIZATIONS

The
LOYALIST
TEAM

LINDA ADAMS

ABBY CURNOW-CHAVEZ

AUDREY EPSTEIN

and REBECCA TEASDALE

with JODY BERGER

PUBLICAFFAIRS
NEW YORK

PublicAffairs
Hachette Book Group
1290 Avenue of the Americas, New York, NY 10104
www.publicaffairsbooks.com
@Public_Affairs

Printed in the United States of America

First edition: September 2017

Published by PublicAffairs™, an imprint of Perseus Books, LLC, a subsidiary of Hachette Book Group, Inc.

The Hachette Speakers Bureau provides a wide range of authors for speaking events. To find out more, go to www.hachettespeakersbureau.com or call (866) 376-6591.

The publisher is not responsible for websites (or their content) that are not owned by the publisher.

Print book design by Amy Quinn

The Library of Congress has cataloged the hardcover edition as follows:

Names: Adams, Linda, 1956– author.
Title: The loyalist team : how trust, candor, and authenticity create great organizations / Linda Adams, Abby Curnow-Chavez, Audrey Epstein, and Rebecca Teasdale, with Jody Berger.
Description: First edition. | New York : PublicAffairs, [2017]
Identifiers: LCCN 2017008172 (print) | LCCN 2017025151 (ebook) | ISBN 9781610397568 (ebook) | ISBN 9781610397551 (hardcover)
Subjects: LCSH: Teams in the workplace. | Trust. | Organizational behavior. | Organizational effectiveness.
Classification: LCC HD66 (ebook) | LCC HD66 .A336 2017 (print) | DDC 658.4/022—dc23
LC record available at https://lccn.loc.gov/2017008172

ISBNs: 978-1-61039-755-1 (hardcover); 978-1-61039-756-8 (e-book)

LSC-C

10 9 8 7 6 5 4 3 2

CONTENTS

INTRODUCTION

When any one of us starts working with a new team, the first absolute truth we share is that every team can be an extraordinary team. We begin by asking each person to describe their best team experience—one in which everything was clicking and the team was working hard, having fun, and exceeding expectations.

Occasionally all four of us are on hand to meet with a team, but more often, two or three of us work together with one client, depending on their needs and our individual areas of expertise. We get together regularly to discuss our work, share ideas, and brainstorm strategies.

One day recently, Linda described a new team with whom she'd just started working. "A team of eight," she said. "And guess how many had to go back to high school to name a great team experience?"

"Four?" Audrey asked.

"No, I'm thinking six," Rebecca said.

Linda shook her head and looked at Abby.

"Okay," Abby said. "I'll split the difference and say five."

"Nope," Linda said. "Seven out of eight had to think back to high school. One talked about his basketball team; someone said softball and another said hockey; and one talked about a high school theater group. But the eighth person? He had never been on a great team. Never. He couldn't name one time when he had teammates who respected each other, trusted each other, and delivered great results. And he's probably fifty years old.

"This man's been in the workforce for nearly thirty years, and he thought the whole concept of a great team is like a unicorn, something people talk about but no one's ever seen," Linda said.

All four of us sat with that for a moment and let it sink in.

"It doesn't have to be that way," Audrey said. "It doesn't."

And all of us agree: being part of a team *can* be a great experience for every team member, but let's be honest—most often, it's not. When we ask people about teams they've been on, almost everyone has a story about a team that fell short. We've heard stories about teams in which every member mistrusted or avoided everyone else, the leader was disconnected, or a lack of communication killed any attempt at collaboration.

We've worked with teams that come close to optimal performance and teams that are worlds away. But wherever a team is on that spectrum, it doesn't have to be (and probably shouldn't be) the final destination.

When we tell people this, they look relieved. When Linda explained all this to the man who thought great teams were as likely as unicorns, he cracked an incredulous smile. Like so many people who serve on dysfunctional teams, he'd been feeling overwhelmed by the experience and had resigned himself to suffering through it.

In the first session with this team, Linda listed a series of specific and concrete actions they could take to improve their performance. As she outlined the process and provided the research to back it up, everyone in the room leaned in to listen as if she were sharing some centuries-old secret family recipe. She guided the group through a discussion to identify their precise goals and then walked them through the steps to attain them. By the end of the day, everyone in the room understood the group's desired outcomes and had a road map to get there. They wouldn't reach the destination overnight, but if they made conscious choices along the way, they would arrive there in the near future. As they learned more about Loyalist Teams, they grew confident that they could become one. And as Linda told us about them, we were confident too.

Even teams that destroy value for the company and create misery for everyone involved can improve. No matter how dysfunctional a team is, there is hope. And we can help.

We have worked with thousands of teams in pretty much every industry and on six continents. The highest-performing teams in any organization and any industry are the ones we call Loyalist Teams. They are the teams that create new markets, lead existing ones, and skillfully maneuver through any and all challenges. The envy of their peers, they create a strategic advantage that's impossible to replicate.

The individuals on these teams are skilled, accomplished, and driven, but what sets them apart is that they trust, challenge, and push one another to exceed expectations. They are loyal to one another, the team, and the larger organization. These individuals work to ensure each other's success as they work to ensure their own. They run toward the tough conversations, not away, and refuse to let each other fail. Team members give honest feedback and support. And regardless of the challenges faced and the hard work required, members of these teams are having fun.

There are teams that may function at this level for a limited time, but only Loyalist Teams consistently deliver extraordinary value. In today's complex business environment, only Loyalist Teams can weather the storms that teams predictably face because they know how to self-correct. They know how to reconsider the options and regroup when necessary.

These teams are rare, but they don't have to be. Every team can become a Loyalist Team. In this book, we will show you how to build and maintain one. We will draw from our research, our extensive database, our consulting work, and our own experiences serving on, building, and leading teams.

CREATING OUR OWN LOYALIST TEAM

We built and operate our consulting firm, The Trispective Group, using the Loyalist Team concept. We believed so strongly in what we knew about Loyalist Teams that we wanted to prove the principles. And more than that, we wanted to live them. We wanted to go all in and commit to each other's success. We even set up our financial model to honor and uphold that commitment. Each of us works with different clients on projects of varying size, but we split all income evenly among the partners. Other firms may track who worked on what and for how long, but we divide every dollar equally among us so that the shared goal is obvious and indisputable.

We started on this road almost twenty years ago when three of the four of us first joined forces and started developing these concepts. At the time, Linda had a track record of success leading HR teams in marquis global companies. She'd built her career and reputation inside Ford Motor Company, Thorn EMI, and PepsiCo. Rebecca arrived with credentials earned through her work with a variety of clients at Accenture Consulting. And Audrey had built leadership and development functions for both nonprofit and corporate organizations. Our different career paths converged at a well-funded technology start-up, Level 3 Communications, where we were charged with creating a world-class human resources and leadership development function.

We worked with really young, green leaders who didn't have a lot of leadership experience but had a lot of smarts. Our goal was to coach, mentor, and provide leadership development experiences that would accelerate their growth. We were a part of their leadership journey. It was incredibly rewarding work.

Rewarding and challenging.

As the start-up's workforce exploded and operations extended around the globe, pressure and expectations scaled accordingly. At the highest levels of responsibility in many companies, a person's time is no longer his or her own. For executives in a fast-moving organization, it doesn't matter whether it's your anniversary or your kid's birthday. If you need to be in Hong Kong, you're in Hong Kong.

Each of us understood that the needs of the business came first for executives, and we agreed to make the personal sacrifices that were the price of admission. We caught the flights to Hong Kong and beyond, competed in the daily "my ideas are bigger and brighter than yours" contests, and endured the episodes of anger and aggression that scar a competitive corporate culture.

Year after year, we put on our game faces and excelled in the workplace. From the inside, we studied the ways in which corporate America functioned and we analyzed the areas in which it did not.

Outside the office, we were wives, mothers, sisters, and daughters whose relationships with family, friends, and communities were built on trust, mutual respect, and collaboration. Those relationships gave more energy than they took.

The more our careers progressed, the greater the divide grew between who we were at work and who we were in the rest of our lives. Bridging that gap became exhausting and harder to justify. The more each of us grappled with challenges and achieved success in corporate America, the more we wanted to live and work in a culture that felt less foreign. We wanted to be our authentic selves with family and friends *and* at work.

In 2008, at the height of the Great Recession, the three of us, each of whom was the primary earner in our families, decided to leave our corporate careers behind and commit to each other. Together, we committed to the dream of building a consulting firm that would support us and our families, while also allowing us to live the Loyalist Team model and teach it to companies everywhere.

At the time, most companies were scaling back budgets and forgoing anything that wasn't essential and proven to impact the bottom line. The market for newly minted business consultants looked bleak.

Still, we believed.

We had built something extraordinary at the high-tech start-up. By acting intentionally, being explicit about what was acceptable and what was not, and holding ourselves and our teammates accountable to those high standards, we had built a Loyalist organization. We knew we could teach others to build similarly high-performing teams and organizations.

We believed in each other, and we believed that what we had to offer would make a difference. We named our new firm The Trispective Group because we would address an organization's needs from three angles: we could coach *executives* to sharpen their leadership skills, we could improve an *organization's* effectiveness, and we could teach *teams* of people to work better together. We decided on a logo for our new firm and thought about creating a glossy brochure. But first, we needed clients.

At the time, Abby was leading the global talent management function at Newmont Mining Corporation, one of the world's leading gold-mining companies. Founded in 1916, the company held tight to a traditional corporate culture—the same competitive, sometimes aggressive culture that Linda, Audrey, and Rebecca had experienced throughout their careers.

As Abby looked to the future, she knew that the culture needed to change, and as an executive at a Fortune 500 company, she could have hired any of the well-known, established business consultants. Instead, she met with Audrey and Rebecca, took a leap of faith, and trusted.

Newmont became Trispective's first client. Immediately, Audrey, Linda, and Rebecca embedded themselves within the organization. The three women brought their passion for building capacity in people and teams. And they focused only on Newmont's success, not their own. Together, The Trispective Group partnered with Newmont to change the culture in this century-old business.

Word spread, and Trispective quickly built a roster of clients that spanned the corporate, nonprofit, and public sectors across North America, South America, Europe, Africa, Asia, Australia, and in one instance, the Arctic Circle. As our business grew, we three partners continued to take care of each other and our clients as Loyalists: We put others' success before our own, we had honest conversations, and we gave the support that allows people to innovate and push boundaries.

Five years into the firm's relationship with Newmont, Abby decided to accept a new role as head of HR for another Denver-based business. She started with endless optimism about the new opportunity and soon realized it was seeped in executive dysfunction and sabotage. Many lived by maxims learned in business school (or maybe on the football field): "Win at all costs," and "Hold your ground, no matter what."

After twenty years in corporate America, Abby knew there was a better way. Like her current partners, she thought honesty and trust could trump bravado. And that collaboration could lead to accelerated, sustainable growth.

Abby wanted to continue the leadership, team, and culture change work she loved without the exhausting exercise of keeping her game face on day in and day out. She wanted to play to win while being her authentic self.

When Abby looked at Linda, Audrey, and Rebecca, that's what she saw. They were exactly who they are. Every day they got to do what they loved and show up as themselves—funny, smart, creative, and multidimensional.

The four of us landed on the obvious solution: Abby would join Trispective as the fourth partner.

Together, we offer a full range of consulting services across a wide range of globally diverse industries. While we consult with leaders in every field, our work has given each of us unique opportunities to find and follow our individual passions. Linda, for example, often works with health care clients, where the stakes are high and the benefits of better teamwork are infinite. In exploring the connection between patient outcomes and effective teams, Linda saw a pattern clearly and repeatedly: when health care teams collaborate more effectively, patients lead better lives.

Audrey likes to take the lead with school systems and other education-based clients. She is inspired by mission-driven individuals and the thousands, or hundreds of thousands, of students who benefit when administrators and educators can leverage each other's strengths and work together more effectively.

Abby thrives working with large institutions that have long histories and are facing monumental challenges. And if there's a high level of complexity to the issues, all the better. Abby's sweet spot is finding ways to tie leadership and team effectiveness to business results.

Rebecca is equally at home in any number of industries where she can work with leaders who feel like they are stuck. She's skilled at getting them unstuck so they can see a new world of possibilities. She excels at connecting the dots and demonstrating how leadership behavior shapes the culture.

With any client, all four of us prefer to work the way we worked with our first client—Abby at Newmont—by embedding ourselves into the team, learning the system, and collaborating with the client to provide the most powerful tools available for improving their performance. And because we develop long-standing and personal relationships with clients, we find different clients respond to each of our different approaches and styles.

Leaders facing really tough challenges tend to respond to Linda's direct but empathetic style. With Audrey, clients can expect to be encouraged to reflect at a deep level on their limiting mindsets and beliefs. She helps them to look beyond any excuses or easy answers to find the exact reasons for the way their team works. For clients who appreciate an intellectual or academic approach to the Loyalist Team concept, Rebecca is skilled at guiding them into what they might consider a "soft topic" in an effective way. And because Abby is constantly considering the strategic business aspects of our work, she affects clients by ensuring they connect healthy teams with better business results.

Since launching the firm, all of us have expanded and strengthened our skills and abilities to deliver extraordinary results for clients. And the reason is simple: we are a Loyalist Team, so each one of us and each client benefits from the full scope of all our skills and wisdom and the synergy that comes from combined forces. As we teach clients, and as we will teach you to do in this book, we share information and resources, we hold one another accountable, and each of us ensures that her partners don't fail.

When we work with clients, we collaborate with them. We join their team and behave as Loyalists, holding them accountable to high standards. Many clients have told us that since they started working with us, they have experienced a period of accelerated growth. New clients show up at a steady pace, and existing clients ask the team to design more programs, coach more executives, and continually expand the relationships.

CEOs don't always hear the unvarnished truth, but they know we will challenge their assumptions, question their conclusions, and deliver honest feedback.

We credit the profound level of trust our clients bestow on us to several factors. First, as women working with an overwhelmingly male population of executives, we offer something separate and distinct from other consultants. The Trispective Team never shows up as ego-driven gurus, with the corresponding air of condescension or a "This is how you do it" set of commandments.

We show up as authorities who care. We know what works and what doesn't, having learned the inner dynamics of team and professional development through decades of study. We trust our abilities and have nothing to prove. And because we're not trying to win the "our ideas are bigger and brighter" game, we don't play offense. Clients, then, can stop playing defense.

When any one of us walks into a boardroom or executive team meeting, she is often the only woman in the room. More importantly, she enters the room absolutely comfortable in her skin and clear in her role. She knows she has the goods to move a team forward, and she knows that is her only goal. Because of that clarity, everyone in the room can relax and participate with an openness that allows for candid conversations and real progress.

The four of us meet clients at the client's point of need and study the team and business dynamic without judgment. We ask open-ended questions and listen. Because everyone in the room—client and consultant alike—knows we are not listening for a right or wrong answer, the client can provide the real data that leads to better decisions and more intentional actions.

We never consider anyone or any team beyond reach. We know that with the right tools and resources, every individual, team, and organization can improve performance. And those tools and resources are embedded in the Loyalist Team concept that we as partners live every day. With clients, we strive to share our passion so others can experience the power and joy of serving on a Loyalist Team. And with this book, we offer the same empowering lessons to you.

In Chapter 1, we will provide an overview of the Loyalist Team concept and introduce four teams that exemplify the four team types. In Chapter 2, we show how we diagnose teams and give you the tools to diagnose your own.

Chapters 3 through 6 are deep dives into each team type. We pick up with the team we introduced in Chapter 1 and add a second team to show some of the diversity that exists within each category. All Saboteur Teams, for example, include at least one person who believes that he or she wins only when others lose. The impact of that belief can vary, and the keys to resolving the problem can differ from team to team.

We also wanted to add teams to answer some of the questions we hear all the time: My team is a virtual global team; can we become Loyalists? Or, I work for a nonprofit and we're all committed to the mission; does that make us Loyalists? And finally, what do I do if I think my boss is the Saboteur?

In Chapters 3 through 6, we answer these questions and give direct guidance for leaders and team members.

The teams in these chapters are composites of real teams with whom we've worked. We've changed the names of people and altered the names and details of each company so we could share the full truth about teams. And we've combined characteristics of various teams in order to show you the best examples and most prominent features of each team type. Also, each of us has worked individually with teams in each of the four categories. Combining actual teams into the composite teams in these stories allowed us to give you the collective wisdom of all four partners in Trispective. And we hope that, after having diagnosed yourself or your team in Chapter 2, you can use these middle chapters to learn more about your team, what makes it function the way it does, and what steps you can take to move toward a more productive dynamic.

We'd been observing teams for years and noting the traits that high-performing teams consistently exhibited. We created an assessment tool that allowed us to quantify and record these traits. We collected all the assessment scores in one database, and when we analyzed the data we were astonished. The traits and characteristics of Loyalists so consistently correlate with extraordinary results that we see no reason for any member of any team to settle for anything less. In Chapter 7, we share this data, and it seals the argument on why you can and should encourage your team to become a Loyalist Team. In Chapter 8, we'll make the case once more for becoming a Loyalist Team, respond to the questions we often hear, and address how to sustain your team once you've become Loyalists.

In our book, as in our practice, we strive to demystify the keys to building a high-performance team because these extraordinary teams are not made by magic or rocket science. After gathering data on these teams for years, we can assure you that the formula works: if you learn and practice the Loyalist behaviors, you will vastly improve the performance of your team.

This is true for every person on every team. Whether you are the team lead or a team member, you can use the action plans outlined in this book to improve your team's performance no matter who's on your team now, the difficulty of the situation, and the audacity of your goals.

So let's get started!

1   THE FOUR TEAM TYPES

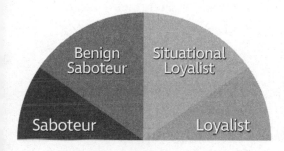

The best teams make it look easy. They perform together so well and so consistently that it appears as if they are one single organism instead of a group of disparate personalities with varied backgrounds. It can look, from the outside, as if skilled and talented people came together and blended their skills and talents effortlessly.

If it were the case that no effort was necessary, building a high-performance team would be as simple as pulling smart people together and saying, "Go." But of course, that's not the case. We all have served on or seen teams of extraordinary individuals who come together and fail, sometimes spectacularly. But the missing ingredient—the difference between the high flyers and the failures—is more than luck or good timing.

Building a high-performance team is like building a stunning skyscraper. There are laws of physics, and rules of engineering. There are also predictable patterns by which teams break down.

From the least effective to the most productive, teams break down or succeed in specific, identifiable, and replicable ways. We've worked with thousands of them, and they all fall into four distinct team types.

WHEN A SABOTEUR ENTERS THE TEAM

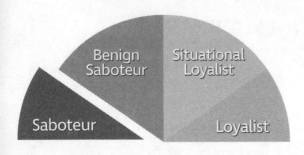

Tim Barnes arrived in California eager to take the reins and lead the Los Angeles office of North Star Financial Services. A Santa Monica native, he'd moved east for college and started his career on Wall Street. Twenty years later, he'd built a solid reputation as a man who could focus a diverse group of people around a common goal to achieve extraordinary results. Recruiters called him often to discuss opportunities in New York, London, and Hong Kong, but none of those interested him.

The opportunity with North Star offered something more appealing: a chance to move home. It was an established firm, and according to the executives in New York, the LA office held a cohesive if slightly underperforming team.

His first week on the job, however, Tim wondered about that assessment.

His first day, he had asked his team to meet in the conference room. "I'm glad we're all together," Tim started, "and to be honest, I don't have a detailed agenda for this meeting. I just want to hear from you, to learn what you all are focused on and what you're excited about."

His new team had no response. Nothing. Tim could hear the clock on the wall.

He tried again. "Really, I just hoped we could have an informal conversation so I can get up to speed on the office, the team, and the business." He looked around and saw a few hesitant smiles, one blank face, and at least one person studying the grain on the table.

"C'mon, give the new guy a hand," Tim said, and looked around again.

Finally, Matt Stone broke the silence. He looked to be about the same age as Tim, with thick, dark hair and deep green eyes.

"I think you'll find that we're all real excited to work with you," Matt said. "As you know, I've been running the office for six months as interim Managing Director, and I think I can speak for all of us. We've built a lot of momentum and can't wait to hear how you're going to keep that going, or add to it."

Tim decided to hold back any response and continued with the same easy tone that he'd started the conversation with. He told the team about his early career, his previous position, and growing up with his mom and two brothers in a two-bedroom apartment just a mile from the office. "My mom still lives here," he said. "I'm grateful to be home."

Tim tried again to generate conversation and received the same anemic response. He shut the meeting down early and shifted tactics, deciding to get to know each person individually. That evening, when the office sounded deserted, he wandered down the hall and caught Jorge at his desk.

"Hey, do you have a minute?"

Jorge cleared a stack of files off a chair and said, "Sure, have a seat."

"Thanks," Tim said. "I'm just trying to get a handle on how this team works. Can you tell me about what you're working on and what you think is going well?"

Jorge started talking very specifically about various projects, with detailed timelines, numbers, and dates. He didn't mention any of his colleagues, so the new boss asked, "What are the relationships like around here, with each other and with New York?"

"Well," Jorge said, "it's been kind of a tough go since the previous Managing Director left. It's become really political."

Tim nodded and said something as simple as, "Oh, really?"

Jorge relaxed a bit more and started talking about Matt's leadership style. "He's on the phone with New York a lot, as far as we can tell," Jorge said. "We don't really know what he does, because he doesn't share information with the rest of us."

Tim nodded again, and Jorge continued, slowly at first. As Tim let him talk, though, Jorge felt more and more comfortable until he finally revealed the real issue. "Honestly," he said, "I don't trust Matt at all. I wouldn't be surprised if he's throwing all of us under the bus or taking credit for our work."

The two men spoke until the conversation felt complete. Tim thanked Jorge for the candor and said, "Let's get home to our families. I'll see you tomorrow."

Driving home, Tim reviewed the easy conversation with Jorge and compared it to the stifled air in the team meeting. The next morning, he started scheduling one-on-one meetings with the other team members. He invited each person to meet outside the office for breakfast or coffee. And over the next week, he met each of his new direct reports and focused on listening.

Each conversation started slowly and built to a set of similar comments:

"We used to work as a much tighter team, helping out with each other's clients. But these last several months, I don't even know what anyone else is working on."

"We aren't much of a team. It's more dog-eat-dog, and Matt thinks he's the top dog."

And, "Now it feels like everyone's just out for themselves. I don't know if I trust anyone anymore. And since they put Matt in charge, it makes me question the whole company."

Tim was concerned but not all that surprised. He'd been down this road before. Although they were clearly in victim mode, at least they seemed sincere about wanting change and looked almost relieved to tell someone what was going on.

At least that was the pattern until Tim met with Matt.

In a diner near the office, Matt couldn't wait to share his insights. "I've been working really hard to hold this crew together," he said. "People are smart, but we have lots of problems with accountability. They just can't get with the program."

Tim took a sip of coffee and asked, "Could you tell me more?"

And Matt did. He had something to say about everyone. No transgression was too small to mention. "But don't worry," he said. "I've got your back. I'll help you work through this in any way I can."

Tim thanked Matt for the offer and went back to the office. He called New York to get a read on why Matt was picked to lead the team in the interim. In a ten-minute conversation, the head of HR gingerly told Tim some of the background and confirmed his suspicions. The executive team knew Matt was arrogant, but they knew he was aggressive too: at least he'd get stuff done.

Perhaps the former director had kept a lid on Matt's more destructive tendencies. Or maybe he tolerated them. Tim wasn't sure. All he knew was that in its current state, his team would not perform at the level he wanted and expected.

Only a few weeks into his tenure, Tim called us for help.

We spent some time with him and interviewed each member of his team. It didn't take long to realize that under Matt's leadership, the rest of the team had moved into self-preservation mode. Each person remained on guard at all times and protected what information and resources each felt he or she owned. All of them had lost touch with New York and the bigger company objectives. They were focused narrowly on their own survival.

Defend, deflect, and protect became the common strategy. And every person—everyone except Matt— was miserable.

Not surprisingly, productivity had nearly ground to a halt. We see this downward shift often when there is a loss of trust on a team. People move into self-preservation mode when they don't know whom to trust. They focus on playing defense and keeping their jobs instead of making forward progress. When we worked with North Star Financial, we saw all the elements and impact of Saboteur behavior: team goals were not met, company goals were not met, and employees were wondering how long they could last.

Sadly, one-fifth of all the teams we see are like this. And we can't always help. While we believe every team has the ability to become a Loyalist Team, teams can only improve if the team leader and all the team members are willing to do the work.

The team at North Star, however, was willing to engage, and we'll pick up their story and tell you more about this Saboteur Team in Chapter 3. And because it's not always a team member who is the Saboteur—sometimes the boss is the problem—we'll introduce another team with a different and equally dangerous dynamic.

A full 20 percent of the teams we see are Saboteur Teams. Usually, people opt out, quit, or find new positions with new teams because surviving on a Saboteur Team is intolerable.

WHEN THE SABOTAGE SEEMS BENIGN

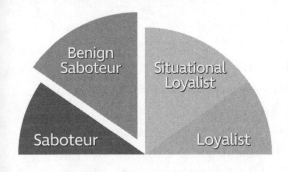

Jane Hu and Peter Thompsen found themselves in an unlikely and uncomfortable situation. The two had always been friendly rivals. As a graduate student at Stanford University, Jane had known and respected Peter's work and even collaborated with him on a research paper. She was inspired by his intellect and liked him enough to joke about how sad it was that he had to study at that lesser East Coast institution.

From his perch at MIT, Peter respected Jane's work ethic and creative thinking. And because she knew that, he could text her from time to time with a wink and a smile. "Jane," he might try, "looks like that California sun is affecting your thinking. You could really contribute so much to the field if you just joined a more rigorous academic department."

The two earned their PhDs the same year and, with their shared interest in computational biology, joined similar if rival firms. Jane joined Gordon Street, another Stanford grad who studied computer science and genetics long before the combination was cool. Gordon was among the first to understand how advanced computing could accelerate the growth of medical knowledge. His firm, G Street Technologies, pushed the leading edge of analyzing genomic research for pharmaceutical companies. Jane served as Chief Technology Officer and enjoyed her role within an aggressive Silicon Valley firm that charted new territory and consistently expanded into new markets.

Meanwhile, Peter stayed in Massachusetts and went to work for a retired MIT professor who had become a serial entrepreneur, launching a new business every three to five years. His firm, MassTech, was small enough that Peter served as head of Operations and Technology. His team moved very strategically, carefully considering every play and making sure every new technology was perfectly dialed in before taking it to market.

Jane and Peter, both hotshots in the field, saw each other at conferences and followed each other's work from afar.

Until they landed in offices on the same hall, in the same building.

As demand for G Street's services grew, Gordon had started looking to acquire a compatible firm so he could expand his capabilities. He thought the CEO at MassTech might be looking to sell and move on. Gordon made the call, started the conversation, and quickly folded MassTech into G Street.

For the first time in their careers, Jane and Peter reported to the same boss and lived and worked in the same city—Palo Alto. And months into the new arrangement, they seemed more like rivals than old friends. Each led a team of talented professionals who came with their own culture. Peter's crew stayed in Boston and wore their best 1990s business casual to work. Jane's showed up in sneakers and T-shirts and shouted over each other at the conference table. Members of Peter's team, who patiently waited to speak in the videoconference meetings, were drowned out. As the company kept growing and clients kept calling, the pressure built. Everyone knew this was the biggest opportunity of his or her career. None of them had failed before, and all were afraid that they might fail for the first time and blow this incredible opportunity.

An undercurrent of tension ran through team meetings and every interaction. At the end of a particularly stressful week, Jane finally went to Peter's office to have the conversation she'd been avoiding.

"What's going on here?" she asked. "Why isn't this working? We're both committed to the work. We both know what needs to be done. And yet, something's not meshing."

Peter agreed with her assessment and didn't have a solution. "I know," he said. "My team and I were really excited about the chance to join G Street, and yet we feel like maybe we don't belong here."

Jane quickly disagreed. "Oh, no, everyone likes you and thinks your team is incredibly talented—we're really glad you're here," she said, "But it feels like we're not collaborating that well. Everyone is staying in their own lane. It seems the Boston crowd just sticks together. Maybe it was wishful thinking on my part, but I thought the integration would be easier."

Peter nodded. "I agree," he said. "It feels like the tensions are brewing and only getting worse. We don't have enough clarity on who owns what. My team is trying to do what they think is right and stay focused at the task at hand. And me, too. I don't want to step on your toes, but at the same time I see so many opportunities for us to do things better."

Later, Peter called his old boss, the MIT professor who had served as CEO on multiple enterprises. "You know," the old man said, "Gordon really needs to step up. You and Jane can't be expected to solve this on your own. You're both buried with work, you've never had to bring two companies together, and you're not getting direction from the top."

Within twelve months of acquiring the rival firm, Gordon saw revenue stagnating and starting to fall. A member of his Board of Directors, a seasoned CEO who had acquired many companies over the years, told Gordon he believed the problem was internal—that Gordon was searching external factors instead of focusing on integrating MassTech within G Street—and the teams were not in alignment yet. The Board Member told Gordon to put more effort into leading his team and suggested he call us.

When we evaluated the G Street team, we quickly realized it had become a Benign Saboteur Team. On these teams, people generally get along. They're collegial. They might go to lunch together. They may maintain positive, perhaps superficial, relationships with one another. There isn't bad intention or ill will. Yet something isn't working.

Everyone knows there's a problem even if they can't articulate it.

When we interview people on these teams, they don't say anyone is actively out to get them. Mostly, they are just siloed and not working together well. People are playing it safe. We see leaders who may not be holding the team to a high enough standard or may be turning a blind eye to intrasquad conflicts.

On Benign Saboteur Teams, team members do what the newly merged G Streeters did: they put their heads down and get their work done. They don't share responsibility for the team's health, and they don't commit to each other's success.

This stay-in-your-own-lane strategy can work for a time, but not forever.

G Street had the sharpest minds in an emerging industry. In Jane and Peter, the firm had two brilliant scientists and strong leaders. Yet with its bifurcated leadership team, this collection of amazing assets was falling short of its potential. The firm was less than the sum of its parts and could not innovate or anticipate future challenges and opportunities. And the company's future was on the line.

In Chapter 4, we'll continue this story with this team, and we'll tell you about our experience with another Benign Saboteur Team.

Of all the teams we see, 30 percent are Benign Saboteurs. Some of them were hurriedly welded together by a merger or an acquisition, as the G Street team was, and some are teams that are hardly connected at all. As more companies and organizations rely on telecommuting and virtual global teams, they increase the risk of building or allowing a Benign Saboteur Team to take root.

WHEN THE LOYALTY COMES WITH CONDITIONS

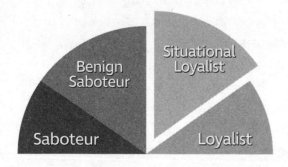

Kathryn Lane always played to win, even as a kid. Her father was a litigator, her mother was a political consultant, and her two older brothers raced to be first down the stairs every morning. To hang out with them, Kathryn learned to deflect pucks, catch baseballs, and shoot hoops in the driveway. She stood five-foot-six but played much bigger, so much bigger that by her sophomore year in high school, college scouts routinely attended her basketball games.

As a senior, Kathryn carefully considered all her options and accepted an athletic scholarship to the University of Michigan. She liked the coach and wanted to push herself academically as well as athletically. She enrolled in the engineering school and, four years later, graduated at the top of her class with a degree in mechanical engineering. Kathryn contemplated playing professional ball in Italy briefly but realized she wanted to stay closer to home and begin a new challenge. She wanted to start her career, and she knew where to go. An industry right down the road offered an opportunity to immediately test her problem-solving skills against real-world problems. Automobiles are not theoretical: they transport people and things from place to place and keep an economy moving.

Kathryn interviewed with car companies, and when her academic advisor suggested it, she interviewed with auto parts companies too. In the end, she received two offers, and as usual, she carefully weighed the pros and cons of each. An engineering job at an automobile manufacturer would be easy to explain to family. It also offered stability and a smooth entry into the working world. Kathryn felt confident that she had the right skills for the job.

ATR Auto Parts offered her a Sales position, however, which sounded like a stretch. It came with more risk and potentially greater reward. Kathryn liked her odds, though, and hoped her engineering background would give her credibility with clients and allow her to talk about products with authority. She liked ATR too, because like the car companies, it had global reach, $14 billion in annual sales, and a long history. Within ATR, Kathryn saw the opportunity to develop a new skill while learning a vital aspect of any business.

Kathryn chose ATR and almost immediately realized she loved working with clients and teaching them about her company's products. And she liked competing against herself—trying to achieve more than she had last quarter and striving to achieve even more next quarter—and comparing her numbers to those of other salespeople and even other companies.

At her first annual review, Kathryn's supervisor praised her for being "organized, methodical, and aggressive," and promoted her to lead the Midwest sales force. Five years in, Kathryn led North American sales for the Detroit-based company.

When Kathryn took on the new role, she quickly promoted Tomasz Budzynski, a fellow Michigan grad whom everyone called Bud, into her old position running the Midwest. They'd had an easy friendship, and Bud could and would call Kathryn any time of day or night with questions and ideas. The two almost talked in code and finished each other's sentences. And Bud wasn't the only one. The rest of the domestic sales team felt equally connected to Kathryn. They called her at home. They called her when they needed support and guidance. They ran their concerns and ideas by her. And in the face of any important decision, each member of the team knew Kathryn could guide him or her to a solution.

Carl Hall, who oversaw sales in the Southern region, was the newest member of the team. And like

Kathryn, he had a strong competitive streak and paid close attention to detail. Kathryn hired him, in fact, after enough people at enough auto shows told her, "You gotta meet this guy. He's just like you."

Carl came with a great track record in auto racing and even better references. NASCAR drivers loved him and said they relied on him to work with their crew chiefs. And Carl hit the ground running with ATR.

Kathryn was pleased to see him reach out to every member of the team. He set up meetings to ask about best practices and explore how he could better engage and deliver. In team meetings too, he was not shy. When he heard something that didn't sit well, Carl would say, "I don't agree. And here's why."

Kathryn could sense hesitation among the rest of her team and hoped it would be short-lived. She knew Carl was a great addition.

About six months into his tenure, Carl flew to Detroit and came into Kathryn's office late in the day. "Can I get some of your time?"

"Sure," she said. "What's on your mind?"

When he started by saying how much he respected his new colleagues, Kathryn knew a "but" was coming.

"It's just that I think our meetings are a show," he said. "Everyone is so polite. We don't wrestle with tough decisions or really delve into them. And I know the company is aggressive and decisions get made, so where does that happen? Where do those conversations take place?"

Kathryn asked for examples, and Carl could describe several, in detail. He started with the decision to kill the intern program. Everyone in one meeting seemed to be on board with hiring interns, but in a subsequent meeting the program had already been nixed with no discussion.

"And the new strategy on corporate partnerships," Carl added. "When did we discuss who would get pulled into that? It seems like it was decided without any debate or conversation."

After the third example, or maybe the fourth, Kathryn stopped him. She'd heard enough and knew he was right.

"Thanks, Carl," Kathryn said. "I appreciate your honesty, and I need to think about this."

Carl had been candid, and in doing so he shined a light on something Kathryn hadn't seen before. She realized that every one of the big decisions he mentioned had been made in her office. Each one was the result of a conversation with a member of her team sitting exactly where Carl had been sitting or, more often, on the phone. It was like the old days, she thought, when she was the point guard dishing to each of her teammates and running the show. ATR's North American team ostensibly played together, but each relied on her for direction.

When she had the opportunity to check in with another more veteran member of her team, she said, "It's great to have a new set of eyes around here. Carl's seeing some challenges with our team."

The response surprised her. "Really? We're good. No need to bring any drama into the equation."

And at that moment, Kathryn realized she needed help. Competitive and committed to the company, she had involved herself in every decision. She had encouraged her team to come to her, but she didn't know how to guide them to be more candid with each other. She knew they trusted her, but the "no drama" comment sounded like sweeping something under the rug and made her wonder how far trust extended across the team.

Kathryn relied on and cared deeply about each of her direct reports. And she worried about what would happen if any one of them decided to leave. Because of that fear, she didn't want to push too hard or insert herself in their relationships. Still, she knew there were communication problems below the surface. If she waited for them to come into clear view, it would be too late.

When she brought us in and we interviewed the team, we found clear signs of a Situational Loyalist Team, which is the most common type of team we see. On these teams, there are deep pockets of trust—what everyone had with Kathryn—but trust is not uniform across the entire team. Often, on Situational Loyalist Teams, the leader is so central and so well-liked that people worry what would happen if she were to leave. Still, Situational Loyalists are more productive than either active Saboteurs or the more passive Benign Saboteurs.

While Situational Loyalists don't always destroy value, they don't create it at the rate that they otherwise might. Men and women on these teams typically know their team is not running as smoothly as it could. They have candid conversations about the dropped balls and missed opportunities with some of their colleagues. And with others, they offer support but stop short of true candor.

When the landscape changes, as it always does in a complex business environment, these teams are not well equipped to adapt and carry on. They don't have all the tools or the necessary commitment to each other to perform at the highest level over rough terrain. Certainly, we see teams that can use a crisis to pull together, but more often, challenges push a Situational Loyalist Team in the other direction, toward the unhealthy behaviors of Benign Saboteur or even Saboteur Teams.

In Chapter 5, we'll pick up the story with ATR, and we'll introduce another Situational Loyalist Team, where everyone was deeply committed to the organization's mission but hadn't learned the mechanics of good teamwork.

WHEN THE LOYALTY IS UNIVERSAL

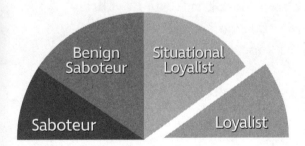

Ian Campbell smiled as the last member of his team packed up and headed for the airport. The annual leadership meeting in Arizona was more successful than he had dared to dream. He'd been the chief executive officer at Torreys Clothing for seven years and had run six of these off-site retreats, and this was the first time he felt completely confident in the future.

With everyone gone, Ian took a moment to sit on the deck and stare at the rugged landscape. "We're there," he thought. "We are really there. All those years of working to build trust have finally paid off. My colleagues and I feel like more than a team. There's no question we have each other's backs. And our results show it. I know without a doubt that we're strong enough to keep charging in this industry."

As he drove to the airport, Ian reflected on each member of his team and how something seemed to shift on the second day of the three-day retreat. One by one, the executives he had hired and groomed and supported started giving each other feedback that was honest and direct in a way he had never heard before.

Peggy Goodwin, the relatively new head of Design, had turned to Helen, the long-tenured head of Sales, and said, "You often fail to include me or my team when making commitments to customers. It puts my team on our heels and we spend unnecessary energy trying to catch up or run recon."

Helen responded angrily at first, but by midafternoon she'd come around and said, "Peggy, you know what? You're right. I will personally commit to working with my team on this. What we're doing now is not effective for anyone, especially our customers."

Ian thought about Manuel Sanchez, the chief information officer and youngest executive, who had acknowledged for the first time that he felt his colleagues, the other executives, treated his staff like the junior varsity. "Look," Manuel said, "we may not be creating the designs or manufacturing the clothing that the public knows Torreys for, but we are integral to this business, and I'd like you to treat my staff with the same respect that I treat yours."

And more than that, what inspired Ian was how the rest of the team responded. They heard the feedback, owned their behavior, and committed to changing it. While they had all talked about assuming positive intent for years, they were really doing it now.

As Ian thought about each person on his team, he realized that each one had revealed something at this retreat that Ian had never known before. They were authentic. They allowed themselves to be vulnerable with their colleagues. Each asked for what he or she wanted, and as a group they put the toughest issues on the table, reviewed the options, and made smart decisions. When allocating resources, they didn't try to determine who won and who lost or divide the pie into equal parts. They made tough but strategic choices that benefited the company as a whole. The leaders whose departmental budgets were slashed were as gracious as the ones whose budgets grew. They all had a company-first mindset.

Realizing this, Ian slapped his hand on the dash of his rental car. "This was a tremendous victory," he said out loud.

As soon as he heard his words in the small space, he was struck by a new thought: "Now we have to keep this going!"

Torreys' leadership team had become a Loyalist Team. Teammates granted trust to one another and began reaping the benefits of a healthier culture and a soaring stock price. They were reaching team goals and wanted to reach a higher level, because they could. They weren't perfect, but they knew how to identify their mistakes and change tactics or behaviors to maintain the rigorous candor and multidirectional trust that are hallmarks of Loyalist Teams. They recognized that maintaining a Loyalist Team is hard work and takes an active commitment to one another. And they were willing to make that commitment.

Where Saboteurs practice selfish behavior, Benign Saboteurs avoid facing the issues. Situational Loyalists go a step further: they're willing to explore the issues, but instead of having candid conversations they may sugarcoat concerns with some teammates or interact with an artificial harmony.

Loyalist Teams go further still. They've explored the issues and chosen to roll up their sleeves and fix the problems whenever one pops up. They call out the "elephant in the room," and they do it with respect. Members of these teams value one another enough to say what needs to be said. They assume that any criticism comes from a place of positive intent—that their teammates want the best for them, the team, and the company, as they do.

In short, members of these extraordinary teams:

- Trust each other unconditionally

- Assume positive intent, and if they can't get there alone, they ask

- Talk to each other, not about each other

- Care about each other's success as they do their own

- Put the team's agenda ahead of their own

- Push each other to do their best work

- Discuss the toughest issues in the room and leave aligned

- Give each other feedback, even when it's hard

When something happens beyond the company's walls—a new competitor shows up, the market shifts, or the economy takes a hit—a Loyalist Team has the commitment, relationships, and practices to keep moving forward. They've built the muscle memory needed to respond quickly. When asked, people who have been on Loyalist Teams routinely report that these experiences were the most positive, engaging, and rewarding times of their careers. Of all the teams we see, very few earn the Loyalist designation—only about 15 percent. But the good news is every team can become one.

Wherever your team is on this spectrum, from Saboteur to Loyalist, you have the capacity for higher, sustainable performance and the ability to become a Loyalist Team. In the coming chapters, we will identify specific behaviors and relationships that need to be addressed and guide you on your path to becoming a Loyalist Team.

2 DIAGNOSING YOUR TEAM

All four of us worked inside corporate America before we came together as The Trispective Group. As Human Resources professionals, we saw teams that ran the gamut from high functioning and high performing to those that were so totally dysfunctional we wondered how they got anything done. Often, we learned, they didn't.

One company we worked with was expanding at an astronomical rate. Increasing demand for its services pushed the company to grow, within just a few years, from two hundred employees in the United States to thousands of employees working in dozens of cities around the world. While the company as a whole looked to be thriving, one specific team and one executive were not. The executive, whom we'll call John, led the Technology function and ruled his fiefdom with an iron fist. He was powerful, confident, smart, and charismatic and viewed any form of dissent as unforgiveable. Other executives appreciated his straightforward, no-nonsense approach. They believed that he was a good leader based on his past success.

Within the Technology department, however, people weren't so sure about him. Everyone knew that disagreeing with John was an act of treason. Even questioning his decisions was read as a sign of discontent, or worse. The men and women who reported to John worked in a fog of fear and mistrust. They, in turn, created the same environment for the men and women who reported to them. Naturally, in this setting, no one spoke freely or felt empowered to be honest with their boss or colleagues. Mostly, people strove to say only what they thought John wanted to hear. To make the situation more precarious, the team was embarking on the biggest technology investment the company had ever made, a complex new IT backbone built on unproven technology. If it worked, it would give the company an advantage over its competitors. If it didn't, the fallout could be catastrophic. The project was a risky bet, and it was the biggest gamble the company had ever taken.

As HR consultants, we heard concerns from people at all levels within the organization. We knew that the team dynamic would sink the project. Over the course of several months, we broached this topic with John. We shared our observations and what we had heard. The developers who were charged with building the technology told their managers that the work could not be done. The managers, however, soft-pedaled it to their bosses and said, "We have concerns about this project." The directors then soft-pedaled yet again when reporting to the Vice Presidents and said, "We have concerns, but we're on it and it's under control." And the VPs and SVPs softened the blow one more time for John, so he heard only, "It's under control."

Beyond the Tech team, there was no communication. Departments that relied on John's team heard nothing at all. These internal stakeholders figured something was wrong because radio silence usually precedes a serious setback, but they were equally hesitant to ask John about it.

We told him about the destructive lack of trust on his team and where we thought it would lead. We explained that team members were unwilling to raise the real issues. We received a familiar response of defensiveness and anger.

"Who doesn't trust me enough to tell me what's going on?" John asked and added sincerely, "Who is it? I'll fire him."

Everyone, it seemed, knew John was marching off a cliff, and no one said a word to stop him or slow him down. Because of his power and his tendency to react first and think later, people were afraid to tell the difficult truth. They rightly feared the consequences to their own careers. Others didn't tell the truth because they actively hoped to see a different set of consequences: they disliked John so much that they *wanted* to watch him fail. Regardless of what it meant for the project or the organization, they wanted to see him humbled, humiliated, and even fired.

Staff meetings were a farce. After our conversation with him, John surprised us by announcing to the team, "Hey, the consultants tell me that you guys don't trust me. If you have something to say, let's hear it now."

Team members—who almost uniformly thought John was the problem—sat silent. No one could say anything because they knew how that story would end. When we explained to the group that we believed they were operating with very little trust, no one agreed or even showed recognition. John, whose frustration was becoming apparent, declared that we must have misunderstood. Team members nodded in agreement. As disappointing as it was, we were not surprised that when pressed by John, they either sat silently or spoke in gentle platitudes.

"We're just under a lot of pressure," one said.

"We have tight deadlines," added another.

"I think we're okay," was the conclusion.

The men and women who worked for John stuck around because of the promise of the business itself and the dream that they might retire early and rich. They hoped they might outlive him. But as they waited for him to fail or the technology to miraculously succeed, they were miserable. Everyone in the department went to work every day feeling he or she was in a no-win situation. None had the satisfaction of a job well done.

The process was wildly frustrating for us. We could see the problem. We could shout it from the rooftops but couldn't get any traction with John or his team. We went to the CEO to share our concerns. "The emperor has no clothes," we told him, "and unless something changes, the project's headed for disaster."

The CEO told us he was on the case. We later learned that the sum total of the CEO's effort was to tell John, "Get it fixed!" With this conversation, the CEO felt the issue had been addressed. He did not want to create waves and risk running John off in the middle of the project. It became clear to us that this CEO, like many other leaders, underestimated the cost of this team dysfunction. Within the team, we could not convince any individual to start the challenging conversation.

Ultimately, we watched this team fail.

After two years of work and hundreds of millions of dollars in sunk costs, the project went live and failed. Not even in beta. It went live on a global scale and failed. Horribly, publicly, and completely. The CEO promptly relieved John of his duties. Many people who toiled beneath him were happy to see him go. But he wasn't the only casualty. Most of his direct reports were let go, and the company as a whole took a hit that would be felt for years. Shareholders saw the value of their holdings plummet. Customers saw their service diminished, and employees saw their early retirement dreams go up in smoke.

Each of us thought long and hard about what we could have done better. We believed then, as we believe now, that every team has the capacity to deliver extraordinary results. And yet, we'd just watched a team deliver disastrous results.

In heated conversations, we considered our role in the debacle and debated how we could prevent similar disasters in the future. We wondered whether we needed new tools or more training. We considered what we knew empirically: that high-performing teams were not made out of magic or by happy accident, that they had identifiable and replicable traits that could be learned and taught, and that every team could move closer to the ideal. We just didn't have a foolproof way to test our hypothesis. And even if our hypothesis proved sound, we didn't have a robust body of evidence to support our knowledge in conversations with clients.

Two things became clear: a Saboteur Team could have a devastating impact on an organization, and we needed an objective tool to provide irrefutable data for actively diagnosing and addressing team challenges.

CREATING THE DIAGNOSTIC TOOL

We set out to find a team assessment that would quickly answer our questions and reveal specific differences between the most and least effective teams so we could begin the process of fixing the issues as quickly as possible. We reviewed all the commercially available assessments and the academic literature at the time. We hired a researcher to expand the search and let us know what, if anything, we were missing. The answer was, "Not much." There wasn't a tool that we felt adequately captured a holistic view of team performance. There was no way to see the distinct traits and characteristics of a team *and* measure the synergy, synchronicity, and friction the team produced while running.

Many assessments provide a 360-degree view of individuals, and there are plenty of personality instruments that can be aggregated for the team. Broad-based engagement assessments could also look at each team to try to determine the team's relationship to the organization at large. We could use a combination of several tools and attempt to triangulate the answers, but that would only give us a sloppy approximation of the information we needed. No single tool delivered the data we sought, so we decided to design our own. We called it the Loyalist Team 3D.

Through extensive research of academic literature on teams, we identified the most critical traits and characteristics of high-performing teams. We developed assessment questions that focused on team mindset, operations, team leadership, and relationships. We also wanted to know how stakeholders outside the team evaluated the team. In short, we wanted micro- and macro-level views of the team's dynamic from the inside and outside.

We created the Loyalist Team 3D to prevent any type of guesswork. A 360-degree assessment, we call it "3D" because it lets us measure a team's tendencies, traits, characteristics, and results from multiple dimensions. By surveying team members and stakeholders, we can answer questions such as, "How much do team members trust one another?" and "How likely are they to discuss the hard topics?" and "How often do team members provide feedback to one another?"

The assessment allows us to design a customized strategy to increase the team's effectiveness for each client. It also lets us hold up a mirror in which the team can see itself clearly, often for the first time.

We tested our assessment with key clients. Like us, they wanted a more detailed view of how their teams worked, and they were hungry for hard data that would show which specific elements caused movement in either direction: toward or away from better performance. We partnered with five client organizations in five different industries to validate our team assessment tool with their employees.

We administered the assessment to thirty distinct teams working in the engineering, hospitality, retail, financial services, and education sectors. We tested our assumptions, analyzed the results, and learned a lot.

The data supported our conclusion that teams exhibiting one cluster of similar tendencies—the traits we now attribute to Saboteur Teams—delivered similarly lousy results. The data also showed that teams with a separate cluster of traits—the ones we now attribute to Loyalist Teams—routinely delivered extraordinary results.

Simultaneously, we learned that some questions we thought would matter revealed no useful information. Other areas of inquiry proved to have a higher correlation to team performance than we had expected. With this new understanding, we revised the tool and re-tested it with a new batch of teams. Over the next few years, we continually reviewed the data and refined the tool until we had something that gave the clear picture that we and our clients wanted.

Even in its earliest iterations, we saw how powerful the assessment was for clients. It allowed us to dig into so many areas of team performance. And it allowed us to present the information in a way that clients could hear. When members of their teams answered the twenty-minute questionnaire and we shared the findings, clients didn't disagree. They didn't say, "No, that's not right." With the data in front of them, no one argued, "Trust? What are you talking about? We trust each other," when they knew they didn't.

Teamwork, which has long been seen as a soft skill, could now be evaluated with the Loyalist Team 3D and reported on with hard numbers. Instead of thinking, "Something's wrong. Let's take the team off-site, play golf, and practice trust falls and hope that helps," leaders could take a much more targeted approach to team building. Instead of picking an off-the-shelf solution and crossing their fingers, leaders could see exactly what was wrong and start there.

As consultants, we use this assessment to dig a layer deeper and really understand the inner workings of the team. The Loyalist Team 3D allows the team to get to the behaviors and actions that define its dynamic. With the assessment, we know if the team is intentionally working on building and maintaining trust. We can see if they are putting the tough issues on the table and if unacceptable team behaviors are called out and addressed. It allows us to get to a specific diagnosis so we can develop the right treatment plan and get started.

With clients, we've seen how the results from the assessment crowd out the noise and let them focus narrowly on the areas that need attention. In its broadest form, the data identifies which type of team they are working on and points to the most critical areas for improving team performance.

One thing we learned early in our work with teams is that one size does not fit all, not when it comes to improving team performance. We make sure our clients understand that, and we explain that each of the four different team types requires a different approach. To solve the problem and increase effectiveness, the team has to know where it's starting.

Saboteur Teams, for example, have much more deeply ingrained patterns of dysfunction than Benign Saboteur or Situational Loyalist Teams. Because everyone on a Saboteur team is miserable and the team is significantly underperforming—picture John's team keeping him in the dark as he sprints toward the cliff—these teams need very specific interventions. And they need them urgently.

The two middle team types, Benign Saboteur and Situational Loyalists, are more passive in their actions and attitude. For Benign Saboteur Teams, lost opportunities abound. No one person is living up to their potential, and the overall level of inertia has to be addressed directly. On Situational Loyalist Teams, members and stakeholders alike are generally happy with the team's performance, so the team needs a strategy to get past the mentality "If it ain't broke, don't fix it!"

Finally, Loyalist Teams, which are at the top of their game, need to challenge conventional thinking and be relentless about reinventing themselves. They need to plan for a world where good today may not be good enough tomorrow.

In short, Saboteur Teams need a turnaround, Benign Saboteur Teams need a wake-up call, Situational Loyalist Teams need a nudge, and Loyalist Teams need to find their next challenge.

With clients, we have every member of the team and its stakeholders complete the Loyalist Team 3D assessment, and we often schedule interviews to bolster the data.

With this book, you can achieve some of the same results: you can determine what type of team you have and the root cause of any dysfunction. And from there, you can start to resolve those problems and move your team toward the realm of extraordinary results.

Whether you're the leader, a veteran, or the newest, most junior team member of your team, you have the power to improve your team. You can get the ball moving by evaluating the current team—its assets, relationships, and shortcomings. And you can effect change. In the same way that one active Saboteur, "the one bad apple," can bring down an entire team, one exceptional team player can elevate everyone around her.

Each of us has the capacity to be either person.

DETERMINING WHO'S ON YOUR TEAM

Before you can get to work on a team's tendencies, and before you can even diagnose the issues facing the team, you need to determine that it is a team.

Not every group of individuals working in the same arena comprises a team. A group of people reporting to the same supervisor can be called a team even when they are working on different projects and have no interaction. We've also seen people misidentified as a team because they are working on the same project but never really cross paths or alter each other's decisions.

In our work, we use a simple definition of team. People are members of a team if they:

- Work toward the same goal and
- Impact each other's behavior and outcomes.

That's it. Two points determine a team.

As you start using this book, consider the people you work with. Ask yourself if you share a goal and impact one another. If the answer is yes, or should be yes, that's a team. And like many of us, you may serve on multiple teams. Even within one organization, most people serve on more than one. A person can lead one team and serve as a member of another. A team can be permanent, like a standing committee or board of directors that meets over and over through the years to guide and execute long-range plans. Or a team can come together quickly to complete one project and disband as soon as the goal is reached. Teammates can occupy one office, or they can live in far-flung places, sharing a mission and meeting only in a series of conference calls or in the virtual world.

All of them benefit from learning to be better teammates.

DIAGNOSING YOUR TEAM

Business leaders measure everything from the smallest details of their operation to the most comprehensive view of the market in which they compete. They know the cost to the penny of raw ingredients, the cycle time to the minute of product development, and the details of their consumers' demands on every variation of every product. They examine the most minute details so they can make decisions based on data. And for most businesses, the number one expense is the people. These people work on teams, and yet business leaders have no way to measure team performance. With the Loyalist Team 3D, leaders can diagnose their teams and take the guesswork out of the equation. The assessment creates a starting point for improvement and a quantitative way to measure change over time.

We wrote this book to give you something similar. Whether you're a leader or a team member, you can use this book to diagnose your team and plot steps to improve team performance. We suggest you start with the team that is most prominent in your work life: either you spend the most hours with this group of people or the team's goal is the most meaningful to you, your career, or your organization.

First, consider that team and ask yourself this series of questions:

- Is the team delivering results?

- What's working best on this team?

- What are the challenges this team is facing?

- Has anything significantly changed with the business or this team in the last six months?

- Is everyone pulling his or her weight?

- How do I affect team performance?

- How does the team leader impact team performance?

- How would you describe this team's reputation?

- How would you describe the relationships on the team?

- How is morale on the team?

- What are the barriers to better performance?

Loyalist Team Checklist

Check the boxes that best describe your team.

	SABOTEUR TEAMS	BENIGN SABOTEUR TEAMS	SITUATIONAL LOYALIST TEAMS	LOYALIST TEAMS
Team Motives	☐ Focus is on personal success ☐ The failure of others is often seen as a path to individual success	☐ Focus is on self-preservation ☐ The goal is to survive	☐ Focus is on the team's success ☐ The goal is to keep things moving in the right direction	☐ Focus is on the team and organization's success ☐ The success of others is viewed as a path to individual success
Team Mindsets	☐ Distrust ☐ Suspicion ☐ Assuming negative intent ☐ My way is right (yours is wrong) ☐ "Watch your back" ☐ "Get them before they get me"	☐ Situational trust ☐ Each for themselves ☐ Playing it safe ☐ False sense of harmony ☐ "Live and let live" ☐ "I keep my head down"	☐ Strong pockets of trust ☐ Benefit of the doubt ☐ Commitment to team goals ☐ Intelligent risk-taking ☐ "We are good enough"	☐ Trust ☐ Assume positive intent ☐ Together we are stronger, sharing experiences and knowledge ☐ Commitment to each other ☐ "We win together; we lose together"
Team Behaviors	☐ Providing negative feedback or inauthentic positive feedback ☐ Undermining others ☐ Playing the blame game ☐ Driving fear and insecurity ☐ Engaging in one-upsmanship ☐ Causing trouble and creating drama ☐ Constantly pointing out what is going wrong (with little acknowledgment of what is going right) ☐ Hoarding critical information from others for own gain ☐ Looking for wins regardless of the impact on others ☐ Gossiping ☐ Making plays behind the scenes	☐ Withholding feedback and information that could possibly be helpful to others ☐ Not visibly supporting others in the face of trouble ☐ Staying within own silo and making limited effort to learn what others need to be successful ☐ Delivering only on defined commitments; may not go the extra mile for the team ☐ Highly skeptical about the possibility of successful change ☐ Waiting for others to engage in any change before making any commitment ☐ Staying silent on controversial issues ☐ Limiting interactions to avoid conflict or commitment	☐ Carefully considering the impact of feedback before providing it ☐ Taking some risk in support of others, even when it's uncomfortable ☐ Strong alliances exist but not equally across the team ☐ Delivering on team commitments ☐ Often "leader-centered"; the leader is essential to team accountability and decision-making ☐ Considering the implications to others before taking action ☐ Meeting others partway; comfortable with give-and-take ☐ Consulting team members regularly ☐ Not engaging in discussions about others if they are not present	☐ Proactively providing candid feedback ☐ Actively engaging in productive conflict to get the tough issues on the table ☐ Sharing accountability for decisions and results ☐ Helping others maximize their strengths; stepping in to support challenges ☐ Unequivocally having each other's backs and looking for win-win outcomes ☐ Sacrificing resources and potential opportunities for the good of the organization ☐ Talking directly to the person with whom there is an issue ☐ Creating an environment where everyone does their best work

Next, look at the Loyalist Team Checklist below. Select the statements that are most reflective of your team today.

The column with the most checks is most likely the type of team you serve on, but the labels are not absolute. You'll have checks in multiple columns because each team can exhibit qualities from more than one type. A Benign Saboteur Team, for example, can show some Situational Loyalist tendencies, and a Situational Loyalist Team can even behave like a Saboteur Team on rare occasions. For the most part, though, this checklist will tell you your starting point.

We also offer a free and simple assessment on our website, www.TrispectiveGroup.com, the Loyalist Team SNAPSHOT that will tell you which type of team you're on and deliver descriptions and next steps. You can take this assessment as a team leader or a team member.

Wherever your team falls on this spectrum from Saboteur to Loyalist, you have the capacity for higher sustained performance and the ability to become a Loyalist Team. The journey begins with a clear diagnosis and proceeds from there. In the coming chapters, we will identify specific relationships and behaviors that need to be addressed for each of the four team types, and we will guide you in your quest to address them. There is no shortcut, and the work is not easy, but it is achievable and worth the effort. With an honest assessment, teams can start building the culture and relationships needed to create extraordinary value.

3 SABOTEUR TEAMS: WHEN BAD TEAMS HAPPEN TO GOOD PEOPLE

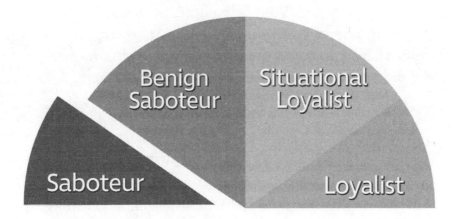

WHEN A SABOTEUR ENTERS THE TEAM

Matt Stone arrived early for his interview. His cufflinks looked sharp, not flashy, and his suit was well-tailored. His smile either exuded confidence or concealed a deep-seated insecurity—it can be difficult to distinguish between the two at first glance.

"I'm so glad Tim brought you in to help," Matt said to start the conversation, reaching across the table to shake hands with us. "This office has so much potential, and lately, we just aren't hitting the mark. I tried to hold this place together, and I did a good job for a while, but wow, there's only so much one person can do, especially as an interim director."

Matt was right: we were interviewing him and his teammates precisely because the Los Angeles office of North Star Financial had great potential that the team was not reaching. The newly hired director, Tim Barnes, had arrived in Los Angeles three months earlier and tried to decipher and get a handle on whatever was going on but realized he couldn't do it on his own. The team was in a downward spiral, destroying value faster than Tim could allow. And he couldn't reverse the slide in time to save the operation without help.

Tim called us because we had worked together successfully at his old company. At the time, he had inherited a team that could not make decisions and members who could barely tolerate one another. In team meetings, they vacillated between lack of interest and disrespectful sniping. We ran the diagnostics and identified the two biggest issues facing the team: a lack of accountability and an unwillingness to deal with conflict. We worked with the team to strengthen relationships and focus on the company agenda rather than fractured individual agendas.

At North Star, Tim hoped we could achieve similar results by first finding the root cause of this team's dysfunction. When we heard him describe the office dynamic, we recommended that we schedule interviews with the team and stakeholders and ask them all to complete the Loyalist Team 3D assessment.

We also requested personality assessments for every individual. Several companies offer different versions of these assessments. Each one has different strengths and limitations, so we use whichever one the client prefers. We have found that these tests help teams discuss differences in approach, style, communication, and decision-making in a way that doesn't feel judgmental. By learning more about their own individual tendencies, team members can start to see that such differences are genuine preferences in interacting with the world and that different styles are not intentional ways to annoy each other.

When all the team members see their individual preferences and those of their colleagues—where they are similar and where they differ—it helps the team improve how it works together. Often team members see each other's preferences and have an epiphany: "Oh, you're not just doing that to make me crazy? That's how you collect information and navigate the world? Got it."

Tim quickly gave the go-ahead for the complete diagnostic, and we scheduled the interviews. We started each one with an easy, open-ended question and heard thoughtful comments from almost everyone. Matt was the exception. He entered the room with his own agenda and started telling us everything he thought we needed to know to right the ship. We stopped his monologue and slowed him down by asking what drew him to North Star in the first place. Happy to discuss his favorite subject, he let us know in great detail about graduating from Penn State with a degree in finance.

"Summa cum laude," he added, before telling us about his first job and his stellar performance there, his second firm and the amazing numbers he posted there, and inevitably a third "wildly successful" tenure at yet another firm. When Matt reached North Star in his career timeline, he said it was an instant fit and that the former director, the man who had hired Matt, was a mentor who taught him a lot and trusted him completely.

"Even before he retired," Matt confided, "I was really running the place. The old man deferred to me all the time. It's why the executives in New York felt so comfortable moving me into the top slot when he left."

We asked what Matt hoped to see in the future and what advice he might give Tim, the new director. Not surprisingly, Matt was equally forthcoming on these questions.

"I don't know what is going on with my colleagues, but at some point they checked out," he said. "This industry doesn't have room for that. They don't seem committed to doing what it takes to get the work done. But you can tell Tim that I'm all in and he can lean on me. I know the ropes and I'm the only one willing to do the work."

In the interview, Matt revealed an awful lot about himself, intentionally and inadvertently. When we compared his thoughts to the notes we took in conversations with other members of the Los Angeles office, we saw a disturbing pattern and sensed a troubling team dynamic. Matt saw himself as the last man standing between North Star and absolute disaster, while his teammates drew the opposite conclusion. They saw him as the driving force toward that disaster.

One of his colleagues was particularly blunt. "That guy would step over my dead body to get ahead. And, come to think of it, he may not be the only one. This place has really changed."

Another teammate said, "It makes me wonder about Tim. He should have fired Matt the day he walked in.

Instead, he brought you in here to talk to the rest of us. Not sure what this says about Tim."

Some of Matt's colleagues, however, agreed with Matt on at least one point. When asked what they hoped to see, they shared his wish that things could go back to how they were before the former director left. They just had a very different reason.

"Our old boss at least kept a lid on Matt," Jorge said. "Matt was always annoying. Don't get me wrong, you know—you've met him—but his appointment as interim director made him impossible. And it really made me wonder about the brains in New York."

Eventually, Jorge divulged his own secret. "Just between us, I'm looking around for other opportunities. It's gotten so bad here that I do as much as I can from home. I hate coming to the office, and I can't wait to leave at the end of the day."

Jorge was surprised that we understood his position. We know from our work with Saboteur Teams that the best team members are a flight risk. The team dynamic is unsustainable because most people aren't willing to put up with it for long.

Interviews with key stakeholders were just as revealing. Executives in New York acknowledged that Matt might not have been the ideal leader, but it was only an interim position. They questioned how much damage he could inflict in such a short time. They thought he might offend people, but they didn't know how frequently—and frankly, that wasn't a top concern.

"We knew he'd get shit done," one executive said, before adding, "but something's starting to stink out there. I don't know what it is, but the numbers don't add up. The projections were overly optimistic, and the results aren't there."

In every interview, we asked people to speak freely, and we promised that we would ensure nothing they shared would be personally attributable. Once we collected the information, we summarized our findings and presented Tim with a three-page report.

And even scaled down and made anonymous, the report packed a punch.

We started, as we often do, with a snapshot of the positives:

- There are strong individual capabilities on this team.
- They care passionately about the business and want the culture to change.

The headlines on the challenges were as follows:

- A lack of trust pervades the entire team.
- Relationships are broken across the whole team.
- Individuals showed a lack of accountability for their own behavior and a lack of awareness for how their behavior impacts others.
- One individual, in particular, was identified as a disruptive force.

Then we summarized what we learned about the team dynamics:

Team members saw themselves as victims who were bullied by Matt and abandoned by the corporate offices in New York. Instead of banding together, they retreated to their own offices and let all their relationships fall apart. They felt disconnected from one another and helpless to change their situation. When pushed to consider possible solutions, they uniformly pointed to the boss: Tim needed to do something.

Breaking this news to Tim was difficult because, like most leaders who call us, he knew his team had problems but underestimated the size and scope of them. Few people imagine that they're leading a Saboteur Team, or that their team ranks in the bottom 20 percent of all the teams we see.

We gave Tim the written report and time to digest it. Two days later, he called.

"Do you think there's any hope to turn this around?" he asked. "Should I just get out now? I can probably go back to my old job or find another firm where the team isn't such a mess."

Tim's reaction wasn't unusual. When leaders, especially when they're new to a team, see the dysfunction and the roots of it spelled out in black and white, there's often a major case of buyer's remorse. But this was too early in the game to consider an exit strategy. Even Saboteur Teams are not beyond hope. Every team can make the transition to something more effective, under specific circumstances.

On Saboteur Teams, the leader must be willing to hold himself and his team accountable for improving team dynamics. He must also be willing to let go of people who are unable or unwilling to make the shift. If there is a Saboteur on the team, it doesn't matter if he or she is the star player or a well-connected veteran of the industry. If anyone on the team is either unable or unwilling to play by the new rules, the leader has to ensure the behavior stops or remove that person from the team. No question and no exceptions.

Tim looked exasperated.

"I have to be the parent in this situation too? I have my own kids," he said.

"This isn't all down to you," we said. "It can't be. Relationships are the most important ingredient on healthy teams, and everyone is responsible for each of their relationships."

The leader has to clearly set out his expectations for how people will treat each other and make the space for the team to work on their relationships. Each member has to look herself in the mirror and examine her contribution to the state of her relationships. Then she has to commit to taking actions to repair and improve those relationships.

In understanding this, Tim said, "I got it. I can hold my team accountable, and if anyone says no, they have to go. When can we start?"

Two weeks later, Tim convened an off-site meeting and arranged for us to lead the session. We had spent several hours with him beforehand, designing the agenda, explaining and reviewing all the diagnostic data, offering our recommendations for the team, and coaching Tim to take charge of the opportunity. The first full-team multiday meeting for a new leader is a one-shot deal. Mess it up, and members of the team become more convinced that nothing's going to change. And the more they believe that nothing can change, the more they behave in a way that makes it true.

Tim had led teams in the past and knew what it was like to be part of a well-oiled machine. He knew that a high-performance team produced results while simultaneously rewarding its members with an exhilarating ride that challenged, inspired, and engaged them in a way that few things could.

After his initial hesitation, Tim was game to make the transition happen here. He understood the stakes, and as the leader of a Saboteur Team that was rapidly burning bridges, he knew he couldn't afford to take half steps or move slowly. With his team assembled for a day-and-a-half team-building session, Tim wasn't going to sugarcoat the story or gently wind up to it.

"I know this team is not meeting your needs any more than it's meeting the company's needs," Tim said. "But I want you to know that I am here, I'm invested, and I care about making this situation better for everyone. I accepted this position and made a commitment to succeed. I'm not letting go of that.

"You have talent, skill, and drive, so I know we have an opportunity here to quickly turn things around," Tim added, looking around at each person at the table. "My hope is that this day marks a new era for all of us.

"And I need each one of you to join me," he said. "For the next day and a half, I need you to accept the possibility that things can and will be better. And I need you to accept your role in making that happen."

Heads nodded. Jorge smiled. Even Matt looked like he believed.

To be effective, team-building sessions like this one must move beyond the smiling and nodding and dig into the mess that no one likes to discuss. To move out of the Saboteur zone, especially, teams need to start confronting the uncomfortable truths. Individuals need to speak with candor about how they've treated one another, what they think about each other, and their attitude toward the work they do. It can be a difficult conversation, so to get it started we helped the team consider what ground rules would allow them to feel safer.

After Tim's opening statement, we led a discussion of rules they could agree to for the remainder of the retreat. They chose to:

- Assume positive intent
- Stay curious
- Be candid in their discussion
- Hold open the possibility that things can be different in the future, and
- Turn their phones off and stay present

Next, we talked about preconceived notions and the mental files that people carry on each other. All of us build these files in our minds and fill them with data about how we know people will act and how situations will unfold.

As an example, imagine one person saw his teammate arriving in the office after him or leaving the office before he did. Every day, the same person was in the office first and last. Chances are, he'd unconsciously drop a note in the mental file that said, "That guy's a 9-to-5er not willing to do the work." And then, as time went on, he'd unconsciously recognize and mentally record actions that bolster that assessment. And with each one, the file would fill with more snapshots of a lazy teammate and build the case for, "That guy's just

Think About Your Files

- What files do I have on my teammates?
- How do those files impact my teammates?
- How do those files impact me?
- Are those files valuable to me?
- What files can I let go of (because they weigh me down and negatively color my interactions)?

lazy. He's not committed. I'll have to do everything myself."

One obvious problem here is that the assessment is based on assumptions instead of knowledge. Without asking the "lazy teammate" about his life, it'd be impossible to know that he was an early riser and worked from home for hours before coming into the office or stayed up late at nights, working where it was quiet and he could be most productive.

And of course, without the conversation, the "lazy teammate" is busy capturing his own data and taking his own snapshots. He may see someone taking charge and think, "What a ball hog. He won't share information, and he's trying to take all the credit for my hard work. If that jerk's going to get all the glory, why bother?"

The "files" give us a shortcut to understand what's going to happen in any given situation, and our brains are wired to act on them. If one person believes his colleagues are lazy, he treats them as if they won't follow through on any project.

If others become convinced that someone won't share information or resources, they stop bothering to ask him for anything. They don't ask for help, and they don't ask if he needs help.

With each interaction, the mental files grow fatter and more permanent as each person fortifies his or her stack of evidence.

When we explained this phenomenon to the group, we didn't ask them to throw away their files. Not yet. We asked them to make some individual notes about what they might have in their files about each other. We suggested they consider how these files might be influencing how they act and react with their colleagues. And we asked that for the next day and a half, they loosen their grip on these ideas. We asked them to hold the files lightly and be open to the possibility that the files were incorrect or incomplete, that there may be more information or another explanation for anyone's actions. We asked the team to consider that people could behave differently in the future than they had behaved in the past.

"Just be curious," Tim said, "That's all I'm asking."

The North Star team attempted to remain open-minded, and at times they achieved it. As we reviewed what we learned about each member of the team from the personality assessments, we could see glimpses of recognition and acceptance.

When Tim explained the preferences that showed up in his personality assessment, it was a telling moment: "Once I make a decision, I expect everyone to get on board, no questions asked," he said. "Gosh, my wife's been telling me that for years. She and my kids love that."

Everyone chuckled at the boss's honesty. His comfort with sharing his preferences allowed others to follow his lead. Two women on the team shared their profiles and immediately laughed that they were nearly identical. And even Matt let down his guard an inch or two and shared some understanding of how his clear preference for being skeptical and challenging others might show up for the group.

"I guess it's no surprise," he said, trying to add some levity, "that I always won debates in college."

Saboteur Teams like this one have no time to waste. When the Loyalist Team 3D identifies a Saboteur Team, we tell clients that they need to respond as if their stock price fell by half or their top clients peeled away for another firm. In this team session, we were ready to dig in and make this team face the truth.

After a midmorning break, we brought the North Star team back together and projected the dashboard graphic showing the four team types. We started with the Loyalist Team, listing its characteristics and explaining that every team could become one and deliver extraordinary results if every member was willing to do the work. We then showed how Situational Loyalist and Benign Saboteur Teams fell short.

We introduced Saboteur Teams and spent more time going deep into the lack of trust and the pervasive sense that everyone was in it only for him- or herself. Next we asked team members to share their personal experiences of times when they were on a Loyalist Team and how that felt. We asked how the experience changed them and their work. And finally, we asked how it felt for those who had worked in a Saboteur environment.

We handed out the comprehensive Loyalist Team Checklist, gave them time to work through it, and asked, "Where does this team fall on this spectrum?"

Jorge spoke first. "I think we used to be a Situational Loyalist Team, with pockets of trust," he said. "Now, though, I think at best we're a Benign Saboteur Team. Live and let live."

"No," Matt said. "I'd say we're a Saboteur Team. I feel like everyone assumes negative intent and that I need to watch my back around here."

"What?" Jorge said. "You think you need to watch your back?" Others groaned and rolled their eyes.

"You have no idea what it's been like for the last six months," Matt said. "I kept New York off all of your asses and watched each of you skip out of here right at five every day. No, you were out for yourselves, and I was the only one holding this place together."

Tim later told us that he had been nervous but was relieved that the real issue surfaced so quickly. In the moment, however, he kept a poker face and stepped in. "Hold on," he said. "Let's think for a moment. Is it possible that this is an example of those files we learned about? Is it possible that there is another explanation?"

Initially, the team resisted Tim's attempt at equanimity. Individuals had been seeing themselves as victims for so long that they weren't ready to let go. A few people gave examples of how they were trying to do the right thing, only to be thwarted by their teammates. The conversation sounded like the "poor me" portion of some sad pity party.

Eventually, with our careful cajoling, the accusations and blame softened into something resembling curiosity and self-awareness.

"Hey, man," Jorge said to Matt, "you're right. I didn't understand all the pressure you were under. And looking back now, I'm not really proud of my behavior over the last six months. I know I've been working in my office with the door closed when I could have offered you a hand."

If team building were a mountain-climbing expedition, that was the crux move.

When one team member shows the route to a better place, others can more readily follow. People will hesitate. They'll take baby steps. They might move forward and then retreat. Progress is rarely a straight line. And it rarely proceeds at a uniform pace. But one person can get the team moving—in either direction. Matt may have started the descent into a Saboteur culture, but Jorge showed he was willing to lead the ascent out.

Jorge's willingness to take responsibility for, and to admit publicly, his contribution to the debacle allowed others to do the same.

The ice broke. The North Star team started sharing stories of where they might have acted differently and talked about behaviors they might have misread. They told each other about the challenges they felt operating with the uncertainly that comes with transition. And they even let slide a few comments that revealed their true frustration with Matt. "Why did New York pick

Matt, anyway?" one person asked. Everyone looked at Matt, and he said nothing.

Over the course of the first day, we still saw flashes of anger and remnants of mistrust. We also saw real attempts to connect and sincere efforts to convey the truth. People were willing to raise their issues with Matt, albeit tentatively. Matt was willing to listen and take *some* ownership. It helped propel the group forward, and we felt that the elephant in the room had been acknowledged. We even saw people laugh and poke fun at themselves and, tentatively, at their teammates. Humor can be a good sign.

Mostly though, we saw shock and amazement when people saw the unintended consequences of their behaviors and how their files had taken on lives of their own. Matt judged Jorge's commitment because he saw him darting out most days before dark. Jorge never mentioned and Matt never bothered to learn that he was leaving at five and still putting in twice as many hours because he was working nights and weekends when his kids had gone to bed.

The team also learned that the teammates who appeared to clam up in meetings weren't just withholding information or checking out. Their personality assessment showed a strong preference for thinking through what they wanted to say before saying it. When anyone put them on the spot, they were unable to fully contribute.

Throughout the afternoon, the group worked to identify the key areas of improvement that could lead to quick wins for the team. And they began to plan actions that would drive those improvements.

On the second day, the team wrestled with the rules that would shape new behaviors and created and committed to a set of operating norms to follow going forward. They considered what they needed and what they could promise.

The document they produced looked like this:

In order to focus on building and earning trust with each other, we each commit to holding ourselves and each other to the following operating norms:

- I commit to your success.
- I will stop using the past as an excuse.
- I will not engage in gossip.
- I will not allow others to talk negatively about a colleague.
- I will talk to the person with whom I have an issue and not about them.
- I will support the decisions of the leader and the team.
- I will extend trust and assume positive intent, and if in doubt, I will ask.
- I will let go of my files.

It was a great start, but not a golden ticket. Norms can serve as a social contract clarifying expectations and enabling accountability. Once the norms are written, people still have to execute on their promises. For members of a Saboteur Team, the execution can be an enormous challenge.

Therefore, as the last exercise of the session we asked all the team members to take personal accountability for what this session and these norms meant to them. Each person wrote down and shared with the group three commitments:

1. The immediate action they will take to show up as a more productive member of the team
2. One behavior they will start doing as part of the team
3. One behavior they will stop doing as part of the team

As a group, they also agreed to meet without Tim to let each other know what they are working on and how they might better collaborate. And with Tim, they agreed to a tactical planning meeting to define key priorities and the resources needed to deliver on them in the next six months.

In our debrief with Tim, we congratulated him on leading such a powerful off-site event and asked his assessment of the day.

"I feel like we moved a lot of big rocks out of the way," he said. "Honestly, we accomplished more than I could have hoped. And still, I'm not sold on Matt's conversion."

We weren't completely sold either, but as Loyalists we assume positive intent and we give the benefit of the doubt. And we know it is a process. Tim said he would do the same and that he would proceed with cautious optimism.

We gave him ideas to make the adjustment real. We advised him to keep the team talking about it and to include the operating norms on every agenda. Teams don't turn around overnight. Even the best teams need to commit to the practice. And we promised to come back and lead a follow-up session in three months.

Three months later, North Star was a very different team.

For one thing, Matt was gone.

"He tried to make the adjustment, but after a few months it became clear that he wasn't willing to put the team agenda ahead of his own," Tim said. "I had a tough conversation with him, but I knew it was the right decision."

Tim recognized that by tolerating Matt's behavior, he had been showing the rest of the team he wasn't serious about this change.

Other members of the team, however, were following through on their commitments. They were checking in regularly on their team norms and holding each other accountable. And the results, while not a complete turnaround, were enough that executives in New York were once again optimistic. While the LA office wasn't leading the entire company, the numbers coming out of LA showed a clear pattern of improvement. And as the team showed steady growth month after month, people outside their office took notice. Prior to our engagement with North Star, no one in New York considered anyone in LA when opportunities arose. Six months later, the executive team started to look more carefully at ways to deploy the talent on the West Coast.

Inside the LA offices, too, people saw themselves and their team differently. Because they had made a

shared commitment, their ability to collaborate increased, and their passion for the work returned. They
started having fun again, and they remembered what
they had always loved about North Star.

When we arrived at North Star, it was clear that Matt
was a Saboteur and that his actions had destabilized
the team to the point where there was hardly a team
left. As the new leader, Tim was able to establish team
norms and set the standard: everyone must live by the
norms or move on. When Matt couldn't, Tim made
good on his word and proved his commitment to the
team. He addressed the problem by letting Matt go.

Sometimes, however, we find that the leader can't
solve or remove the problem because the leader *is* the
problem. Saboteur Teams can manifest in many ways.
Wellington Oil & Gas is another example.

WHEN THE BOSS IS A SABOTEUR

A few years ago, we got a frantic call from Wellington's
CEO. Rich Burns had been a coaching client of ours
early in his career, and when he called this time, he
unloaded almost immediately.

"I have two execs at loggerheads," he said. "They're
both smart, skilled professionals who should know better, and yet they keep taking swings at each other. I've
told them a dozen times to get over themselves. I've
told them to go get a drink and work it out. At this

point, I'd let them duke it out, but it's the people on their teams who keep getting black eyes."

Wellington was a Fortune 200 company with drilling operations in North and South America and the Middle East. From the outside, it appeared to be a well-run machine that moved swiftly to capitalize on any and all opportunities. Internally, however, geologists and engineers would tell you that the company could lurch forward only after a series of shouting matches and slamming doors.

The root of the problem, Rich explained, was that his SVP of Exploration and Development, Steve, despised the SVP of Operations, Aziz, and wanted him out. Aziz, in turn, felt Steve was a reckless cowboy who'd take risks that could run the company into the ground, if given half a chance.

"I've run interference between these two for about as long as I can," Rich said. "And I'm through. We've already lost two good people, and we're at risk of losing a third."

We weren't surprised. When a team leader is a Saboteur, the team doesn't stay together for long. People leave on their own or are asked to leave. While not the case here, if the Saboteur is also the CEO, it really doesn't last long. With a Saboteur in the top job, the organization fails to deliver on its promise, so the Board often replaces the CEO before too long.

When two executives are engaged in a Saboteur relationship—as we saw with Steve and Aziz at Wellington—the teams they lead inevitably suffer, and often the team they serve on together does too.

When we asked Rich what effect the relationship between Steve and Aziz had on the executive team, he shrugged it off as more of an annoyance than anything serious. We knew that couldn't be true. And when we asked about the cause of the tension between the two men, Rich didn't have much to say there either. He didn't know what started the conflict initially or why it continued. We didn't need to hear about every skirmish in this long-running battle, but we needed more than Rich could offer. We suggested we set up interviews with the two executives and members of each of their teams.

Rich agreed, and we got to work. James was the first phone call. An earnest geologist on the Exploration and Development team, he'd been with the company five years and had started looking and even talking to recruiters.

"I like my job," James said. "I like the company. I like Rich. I even like my boss, Steve, but he can be juvenile in the way he treats other people, especially Aziz."

Aziz ran Operations. Steve ran Exploration. And the two clashed visibly, according to James.

"If Aziz says something in front of both teams, Steve will tear it apart later when it is just our team," James said. "Steve's constantly denigrating the guy. I don't know why. Aziz seems pretty sharp."

When we talked to Jordan, an industry veteran who reported to Aziz, we heard more of the same.

"We'll all be in a meeting, and Steve will give clear direction on how he wants us to proceed," she said. "Afterward I'll need to reach out to someone on Steve's team to do my job, but Aziz will say, 'Hold off on that.' If I ask why, he'll give me some answer, but basically I know he just doesn't trust those guys. It's really frustrating."

Other interviews uncovered similar disappointment. Nearly everyone said they liked their own teammates and members of the other team but felt blocked from collaborating across the aisle. Most hated the situation and wished their bosses could get it together. A few felt pushed to distrust the other team.

"Personally, I like everyone in Ops," a member of the Exploration team said. "But as a loyal soldier, my boss's enemy is my enemy. I don't share with the Ops team unless I have to."

When we talked to the team leaders, there was no surprise that each blamed the other for the animosity. Of the two, Steve was more animated and eager to dismiss Aziz.

"Listen," he said, "I've been doing this a long time. I'm responsible for finding oil and gas, and we're a goddamn oil and gas company. Exploration and Development *has* to happen, and Aziz can find a hundred reasons to say no to any and all of it."

Pressed to go further, Steve said he knew Rich was unhappy about the situation but didn't need us to intervene. "It's not that big a deal," Steve said. "Some tension between Exploration and Ops is natural. It's healthy, even—keeps us all on target."

In consulting with leaders in various industries, we've heard this line of thinking more than once. Executives who run different areas of the business or directors who lead separate divisions sometimes feel that competition within the company is a good thing. They believe that battling over resources or coming to blows over strategy can bring out the best in their people and put the most creative solution forward.

On one level, it's true: Competition can be healthy within an organization as long as it exists among people who share mutual trust and respect. Heated debates can be productive if everyone is clear on the ultimate goals.

With Wellington, neither was true.

The rift between Steve and Aziz started as a healthy push-pull between the two executives. In their early days with the company, the two execs would disagree, and then, when they were unable to resolve the issue themselves, they'd take it to the CEO. Rich would listen for a few moments, make a quick call, and send Steve and Aziz back to work. Rich's actions kept things moving, but they didn't help the team dynamic among the executives—and they didn't serve Steve or Aziz.

The two men developed a learned helplessness instead of a good working relationship. And they set up a vicious cycle that restarted whenever Rich sided with Aziz and shot down a project Steve proposed. When Steve felt he had lost a battle, he'd come back almost immediately to propose a second, even riskier project. Steve hoped that if Aziz was faced with the two options, he'd regret saying no to the first and reopen the conversation with Rich.

That's not what happened.

"After a while, he was throwing so much garbage over the wall," Aziz said when we interviewed him, "that I didn't even look too closely. Whatever Steve suggested, I was prepared to say no. I own the P&L;

I'm responsible for it; I manage it; and I'm not letting this company take on unnecessary risk to feed Steve's ego."

His remark was telling. We knew then that this situation was years in the making and couldn't be unwound in a day. We also knew that this was a Saboteur relationship that was inevitably holding the executive team back. That team, however, functioned on some level because Rich would continually step in to force decisions so the company could lurch forward. It wasn't an ideal use of Rich's time and talent, but he was the boss and had the power to circumvent the dysfunction between Steve and Aziz.

The teams the two men led did not.

Witnessing the dysfunction at the top, members of these teams adopted the same behaviors we see on other Saboteur Teams. In an atmosphere of mistrust and insecurity, people stayed in their own zones and didn't take chances.

We huddled to discuss our findings and drafted a quick summary to review with Rich.

Steve and Aziz are engaged in a Saboteur relationship, which causes:

- A lack of clarity around goals and priorities for both teams
- Sloppy handoffs between the two teams
- The loss of talent and an increased risk of more departures
- Extensive frustration among team members
- Loss of respect for and trust in the executive team

- Gridlock at lower levels when the two leaders challenge each other's decisions
- A cycle of learned helplessness when Rich steps in to solve their problems

As next steps, we suggested that Trispective would:

- Meet with each leader to review our findings
- Meet with the two men and Rich to review the impact of their behavior on their teams and the company, to determine what Steve and Aziz are prepared to own and their commitment to changing the dynamic, and to make clear that the current dynamic will not be tolerated
- Facilitate a team session with Rich, Aziz, Steve, and both teams to establish a new pattern

The desired outcome is that Steve and Aziz repair their relationship, which will allow:

- Rich to step out of the middle
- Steve and Aziz to come to agreements on setting priorities, resolving disagreements, and sharing information
- A show of unity to the teams
- More effective collaboration
- Reduced tension and unproductive friction between the teams
- Faster decision-making

In a brief but pointed phone conversation with Linda, Rich signed off on the plan. "Yeah, get it done," he said. "I've already spent too much time babysitting those guys."

Within a few days, we crossed off the first item on our list of next steps. We met individually with each leader and shared what we'd gleaned from the interviews. Both men were surprised to see how clearly their teams saw the dysfunction. We weren't: there's no hiding when you're in charge.

Both men were also distressed to see how their behavior impacted the teams. And their responses were telling. Steve said, "I don't want my team to think I'm the bad guy here."

And in a separate conversation in a separate room, Aziz said, "Oh, man, we gotta fix this. What do we do?"

When we moved on to step two—the meeting with Steve, Aziz, and Rich—Rich took charge almost immediately.

"Damn it, guys, this isn't the first time we've talked about this, but it will be the last time," he said. "I can't allow either of you to continue here if we can't get this fixed. This fighting is unacceptable, and I'm tired of refereeing. I'm responsible for allowing this to continue as long as it has, and I'm sorry for that. Going forward, I'm looking for a definitive plan around how you are both going to work together more effectively.

"Trispective is here for you as a resource," he added. "Make good use of them, and I'll expect to meet again regularly to see how things are progressing."

Steve and Aziz mumbled apologizes and promised that the situation would get better fast.

Rich said, "It better," and left.

The rest of us stayed to continue the conversation. We didn't want to spend a lot of time talking about how they got to this point, but we needed Steve and Aziz to get real about the situation and its impact. We asked each of them to imagine the other's point of view.

Steve started, "I don't know how we got here, Aziz. You probably think I'm just a jerk."

Aziz waited as if it might be a trick question.

"There's a lot of failure in oil and gas exploration," Steve said. "It's expensive and I hate to fail. I hate to let others down. I'm under a lot of stress, and I don't always handle it well."

Aziz said he understood. He felt the pressure too.

They each experienced the stress of high expectations in a volatile industry, and there was something else. They each felt pulled in two directions. As they talked more about this, their complaints sounded familiar. Most people in most organizations serve in more than one capacity, as Steve, Aziz, and their team members did. And few people know instinctively how to serve both teams equally. Fewer still understand how their interactions with one team influence the other. When we explained the Loyalist Team model to Steve and Aziz, both men swore they were Loyalists to the teams they led.

"Everyone in Operations knows that I am committed to their success," Aziz said.

"Same for Exploration," Steve said. "My team knows I have their backs no matter what."

Both men believed what they were saying, but we heard otherwise in our interviews. People on both teams said that when they saw their boss treating a peer with disrespect, it raised this obvious question: could he really have anyone's back when he could abandon a peer so publicly?

And more than that, members of the Exploration team needed to collaborate with members of the Ops team to do their jobs successfully. The opposite was true too. If the team leaders were doing anything to prevent the teams' success—including blocking necessary connections—the bosses weren't being Loyalists. They couldn't be Loyalists as long as they engaged in Saboteur behavior with each other.

Team members could see this but weren't sure what to do. They didn't want to make an end run around their boss to collaborate with "the enemy," and they didn't want to let responsibilities drop.

In this situation, when a team member knows the team leader is holding the team back, we counsel the team member to get closer to the leader, to develop a relationship of trust so they can open a dialogue and influence the leader's behavior. We understand the reasons a team member might have the opposite instinct and want to duck and cover, cross their fingers, and hope it all goes away. And sometimes, waiting it out is the best strategy. But if there is any opening with the boss, we encourage team members to develop a Loyalist relationship with that person so they can help change the situation. The impact won't be immediate, but it has a chance to be long-lasting.

At the same time, we encourage leaders, like Steve and Aziz, to take a much more direct approach. In our meeting with the two of them, we explained what had to happen next. We told them to try harder in day-to-day work to see each other's side. Difficult as it was, each man had to extend trust to the other and believe that both were working in what they believed was the best interest of the business. And they had to agree to change their relationship for that best interest of the business.

In a long and at times tense conversation, we steered them to come to agreements on how to set priorities, how to get information back and forth, how to disagree, and when to take the conversation up a level to the CEO.

"So you're saying that if we disagree, we have to work it out between us and not let our teams know?" Steve asked.

The short answer was yes. We explained that they needed to present a unified front to their teams and encourage everyone to collaborate. They each needed to let their teams know the water was safe—no one would be punished for working with the other. People could challenge each other and conflict could arise, but there were no enemies inside Wellington.

Aziz nodded, but Steve looked hesitant. He thought his team would be suspicious if suddenly he and Aziz appeared to be tight. And he was right. Before anyone would buy the new order, the leaders had to meet with their teams and acknowledge the past. They had to have a mea culpa moment and own their contributions to the dysfunctional relationship. And they each had to apologize for having the rocky relationship—to Rich and to each of their teams.

The follow-up meeting with Rich went as we expected. The CEO liked things to move fast and was uncomfortable with anything that smelled like emotion. He listened to their apologies and was ready to push them out the door when Aziz stopped him.

"Here's the thing," Aziz said. "We need you to hold us accountable. If we come to you to resolve our conflict, we need you to say no. We can handle it."

Rich nodded and said that'd be no problem. He'd thought all along that this would be a simple problem to fix, and while we hoped that was true, we knew it wouldn't be. These were entrenched patterns—Rich's role included—and all three of them needed to practice holding each other accountable.

A few days later, we facilitated a working session with Steve, Aziz, and the members of both their teams. Both leaders spoke eloquently about seeing the error of their ways. Both apologized in heartfelt tones for causing confusion and creating an atmosphere of mistrust.

We divided the room into small cross-functional breakout groups and asked them to work together to identify clear points of contention and discuss how information would flow and how issues would get resolved or escalated. We asked them to determine clear points of handover or who would own the decision. They also talked about what had been getting in their way and what they could do differently. At this point, they had specific requests for Steve and Aziz.

"Let us do our jobs by getting out of the middle," James said. "I think we've got strong relationships, and over the past several months we came together to address the safety issue that happened in the field. The two teams worked together to investigate it, conduct a postmortem to determine the cause, and assure that it wouldn't happen again. We can handle things on our own, and if we need you, we'll let you know."

Steve and Aziz acknowledged their part in repeating the cycle of learned helplessness they'd practiced with Rich, and they agreed to let this one go too.

As the session wound down, Aziz stood and spoke first. "I think I speak for both of us when I say thank you—for all your hard work and for not holding back. It wasn't always easy to listen to, but we hear you loud and clear. To all of you and to Steve, I am genuinely sorry for my part in this mess. And I am committed to the changes I need to make."

Steve paced for a few moments before he spoke. "This afternoon was tough," he began. "I can only echo what Aziz just said. We will not go back to how things were, and we need you to hold us accountable and keep us honest. It's a new day around here."

We looked around the room and saw optimism and a healthy sense of skepticism. Team members were withholding judgment and wondering, "Will this stick?"

And so were we. We were delighted that the two men acknowledged their mistakes and promised to behave differently in the future. They each spoke with conviction, but we've learned that there's always a sense of conviction in the moment. People want to do the right thing. And old habits are hard to break.

Over the next three months we agreed to meet with Aziz and with Steve to provide coaching support. We also planned to return at the end of that period to take the pulse of each team. We left the Wellington offices optimistic, but cautiously so.

CLIMBING OUT OF SABOTEUR HELL

Saboteur Teams are destructive, unhealthy, and miserable. Over the long term, they destroy value for their organization.

You know you're on a Saboteur Team when:

- You spend as much time watching your back as doing your work

- People make plays behind the scenes, undermining and sabotaging one another

- Suspicion and mistrust pervade every interaction; it seems like everyone has a personal agenda

- You avoid working with teammates and dread team meetings

- You believe others want you to fail

- Teammates gossip and tell stories about one another

- Bad behavior and poor performance are left unchecked

- There are destructive cliques and factions

- Team members feel like "failures" because they cannot work through the dysfunction to deliver results

Saboteur Teams can't deliver sustainable results because:

- Morale suffers and good people quit

- Strong candidates don't join the team because of its bad reputation

- Critical problems don't get addressed because no one feels safe bringing up tough issues

- Decisions are made covertly or seem highly political

- There's little to no risk-taking or innovation

- Personal and team development are non-existent

- Team members cannot focus on their work

If you lead a Saboteur Team . . .

1. Own it.
If you don't acknowledge that you lead a Saboteur Team and take full ownership for fixing

it, nothing will change. Reflect on how you got here. Think about what you did to allow this dynamic and what you didn't do to address it.

2. **Study the facts and seek out the truth.**
Use data and feedback to figure out what is really happening on the team. Get others' perspectives. Ask questions and be curious. Consider completing the Loyalist Team 3D.

3. **Set new standards and make tough decisions.**
Set new standards for performance and behavior that apply to all team members. Bring the full team together to identify team norms. And make sure everyone agrees to live by them: it takes only one Saboteur to create a Saboteur Team, so if you let one person pass, you're letting the whole team down. Remember, you get what you tolerate.

4. **Get the team on board.**
The team needs to meet regularly, and you need to keep everyone committed to the rules of the road. If you need to, find a strong facilitator to help. That person could be a professional facilitator, an internal HR business partner, or a trusted colleague who has skills and is viewed as being neutral.

5. **Don't give up.**
Turning around a Saboteur Team may be the hardest work you will do as a leader. It takes time and courage. Keep your vision in front of the team while continuing to give team members feedback. Make sure the team

meets frequently to talk about progress and challenges. Remove team members who aren't willing to change.

If you are a member of a Saboteur Team . . .

1. Start with yourself.
You don't need a Loyalist Team around you to start being a Loyalist. No excuses and no waiting for others to change. Try to influence your boss with regard to the high cost of the poor team dynamic. Share your desire to improve the team and ask how you can help.

2. Take the high road.
No matter what, don't engage in gossip about team members. If you have issues with a teammate, talk directly to that person, not about him or her. Don't allow others to gossip with you. Challenge your teammates to address disagreements head-on.

3. Put the team agenda first.
Whenever possible, let the team know that you are a team player and will do what's best for the team, not for yourself. Don't add to destructive conflict and ego-driven debate. Help the team assume positive intent.

4. Own your relationships.
If you have a Saboteur relationship with anyone on the team, including the team leader, take responsibility. Sit down and apologize for your part, clear the air, and reset expectations.

Assume positive intent when misunderstandings occur.

If you suspect that your boss is a Saboteur, it's doubly important to get close and be a Loyalist to that person so that you can influence his or her behavior.

5. **Take care of yourself.**

Saboteur Teams can damage your physical and emotional health. Own what you can, let go of what you can't influence, and make a change if you have to. If you have tried to develop better relationships with a Saboteur boss or colleagues and it's going nowhere, consider raising your concerns with an HR professional or looking for a new opportunity outside the organization.

People who serve on a Saboteur Team or work downstream from a Saboteur relationship generally suffer from the experience. The pain provides strong motivation to move the team forward, but the work is not easy. We don't lie to our clients, and we're not going to lie to you: rebuilding relationships and developing new habits take a lot of energy and courage. Teams need to be intentional in their efforts, and they need to invest significant time and attention to achieve a better outcome.

We've had experience with Saboteur Teams who fully engage and leapfrog from Saboteur to Situational Loyalist. Most, however, become Benign Saboteurs first. And for all Saboteur Teams, things may feel worse before they get better, but the investment is worth it. Instead of feeling like helpless passengers along for the ride, team members who make the investment will gain a sense of control. The journey will not be over if they become Benign Saboteurs or Situational Loyalists, but their work experience will become easier and more enjoyable.

4 BENIGN SABOTEUR TEAMS: HOW TO HURT THE TEAM ACCIDENTALLY ON PURPOSE

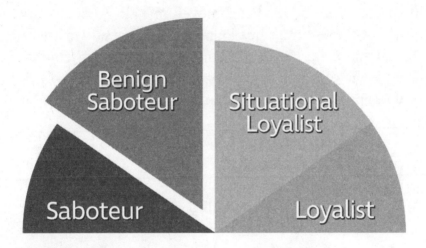

WHEN THE SABOTAGE SEEMS BENIGN

Gordon Street called and wasted no time getting to the point.

"I don't get it," he said. "I have the smartest scientists and engineers working for me, but we're not achieving what I know we can."

Only a year before, Gordon's firm was on the leading edge of computational biology. G Street Technologies was the first and oftentimes only choice for pharmaceutical companies seeking genomic analysis. If anyone had asked at the time about the challenges G Street was facing, Gordon would have mentioned only one: too much demand for their work. And he figured that problem had been solved when he acquired his closest competitor, MassTech.

The acquisition happened swiftly and relatively easily because G Street's Chief Tech Officer, Jane Hu, and her counterpart at MassTech, Peter Thompsen, had long been friendly rivals who knew, liked, and respected each other. Peter moved to Palo Alto to work out of the G Street headquarters and agreed with Jane that his team could remain in Boston to collaborate with the full team by videoconference and email. Gordon appointed Peter and Jane to co-lead the Technology organization.

"I'm not sure what's wrong," Gordon said. "The combined talents should be more than the sum of our parts, and at this point, together we're not. We're much less than the sum. We're behind schedule, and we have to keep revising delivery dates. It seems like our priorities keep changing, and no one is clear who is accountable when issues arise. One of my board members suggested I call you."

We asked for more information about his company: What did he hope to accomplish with the merger and what obstacles did he see in achieving those goals? What were key challenges? And what attempts had he made to resolve them? Gordon answered the first questions easily. On the attempts to solve the problems, though, he drew a blank.

"I'm not sure what Jane and Peter have tried," he said. "I know they're both working incredibly hard. Same for everyone on the team. They deserve better outcomes. And so do our clients."

We hear this kind of thing often. CEOs spend a significant portion of their time focusing externally on shareholders, banks, customers, and the Board. As a result, they may not be operationally or internally focused. Because they hired good people, they expect them to be doing good work with limited input, and thus may lack insight. All CEOs, however, have to understand the culture of the company. They have to take responsibility for the quality and effectiveness of their leadership teams.

Gordon echoed other CEOs we'd worked with when he said, "I don't understand why really smart people can't just figure it out."

We told him what we tell all potential clients. Good data helps. Even the smartest people cannot identify and solve inefficiencies in team dynamics if they can't pinpoint the problems.

A data-driven approach takes much of the emotion out of the discussion. It brings into focus and clarifies the team behaviors that are working. We explained our diagnostic process and recommended that we start by interviewing members of the team and key stakeholders.

As we talked through the details, Gordon hesitated. He asked about us, who we worked with, how we worked, and what metrics we had to show our success. We explained that we'd worked with hundreds of teams in all industries and had compiled a robust database on team traits and characteristics and how they correlate to productivity. We explained that extraordinary teams follow a distinct pattern that is both identifiable and replicable. By running our diagnostic on his tech team and comparing the results to the database, we could give very specific direction for his team.

Gordon relaxed at the sound of evidence-based advice but remained reticent.

"Look," he said, "I've got a dozen people who are off-the-charts genius. Have you worked with scientists before? And what would you plan to do to help them?"

"Yes, we have worked with scientists," we told Gordon, "and it's premature to determine a strategy at this point."

Gordon agreed to let us conduct the interviews and said he would decide on next steps once we reported our findings.

And the interviews, as they always are, were enlightening. When we requested time with Jane, she gave us a few options. "We could meet at 7 in the evening or before everyone gets in," she said. "Once the office gets humming, I'm right in the thick of things."

We chose the early appointment and found her in her office with a fresh cup of coffee. Like her boss and longtime mentor, she needed no time to jump into the conversation.

"I'm really impressed with the talent that joined us from MassTech," she said. "But they operate in such a rigid fashion. We're like a jazz band or a jam band, riffing off each other and improvising, and they're like, I don't know, a marching band."

When we pushed her to say more about where she saw the differences, Jane went straight to team meetings—the bicoastal videoconferences where each office appeared to the other as a two-dimensional image on the wall. Jane talked about her original team—the men and women she hired at G Street—as if they were family, and a big family at that, one that didn't hesitate to shout over each other, critique each other's work, or ask for help when necessary.

"Sometimes the meeting will be going on for a while," she said, "when I realize that we haven't heard much from Boston. I'll look at the screen, and it's not that they look horrified but maybe just not engaged, like they're wondering, 'What are you people doing?' I think the world of Peter, and I worry that our communication style frustrates him and his team."

We were curious about the impact this was having on the work. Jane quickly rattled off a list:

- We're not sure who owns what.
- Handoffs are sloppy and uncertain.
- Meetings and discussions resemble scenes from the movie *Groundhog Day*.
- We're not sure who decides what.
- We miss deadlines.
- Priorities shift without everyone being on the same page.

Later that same morning, when we went to Peter's office, he said, "Let's sit and talk upstairs." He saved the file that was open on his desktop, turned off his cell phone, left it behind, and showed us the way to the rooftop deck.

"As you might know," he started, "Jane and I have known each other a long time. And of course I knew of Gordon. He's a legend in this field. It's a privilege to work with them, and the team they assembled too. A lot of brainpower down those stairs."

We could tell he had more to share, so we waited.

"They're brilliant," he said, and slowed down, as if searching for the right words. "I just wonder if they take unnecessary risks. They fly so fast and don't seem to step back and consider how choices will play out. Sometimes one of them will call me at 10:30 at night, and I always wonder why it couldn't wait until the morning.

"My team too, back in Boston, it drives them crazy when they see an email sent at midnight scheduling a meeting for the next day." Peter shook his head. "My guys like to show up prepared. And last-minute meetings don't give them the chance."

As we talked to Peter, we learned that he had been really excited about the merger. He echoed sentiments we heard from Jane about the talent that existed within both companies and the potential he saw in the combined team.

"You gotta know," he said, "I think all of us studied as hard as we did for as long as we did because we believe that applying advanced computational models to the human genome will change the way we understand disease. Back before the merger, when I thought about G Street and MassTech moving together, I thought 'Oh, man, this is it. We are going to find cures and solve real-world problems.'"

Peter shook his head. "That's just not the way it's going."

We asked Peter about how the clash of cultures affected the business, and he had his own list:

- Things change after we've reached an agreement.
- I'm not sure we are aligned on work processes.
- We make decisions without all the information or input from Jane's team.
- We've missed some key commitments.
- We don't spend enough time planning.

When we interviewed people who reported to either Jane or Peter, we heard similar disappointment. Members of the Boston staff felt frustrated by meetings that didn't seem to end with clear marching orders. "I'm never sure who owns what afterward," one said. "I always have to call Peter to double-check."

A member of Jane's team felt that everyone was so afraid of stepping on toes that the two teams weren't mixing it up. "When these two teams got together, there should have been fireworks," she said. "Instead, all the energy just fizzled."

Several members of the team spoke about Gordon. Everyone agreed with his reputation as a leader in the field, but the respect was muddled with disappointment that they didn't see or hear more from him. One Bostonian said, "I know he has a lot on his plate and is spending a lot of time with the bankers. But we could move faster if we understood his vision, priorities, and expectations."

Once we completed the review, we analyzed our notes and wrote a report that kept everyone's comments confidential and shared the big themes. We started with a snapshot of the positives:

- Deep technical expertise
- High level of respect for the work and intelligence of others
- Belief in the talent across the organization at all levels. We have the best and the brightest
- Strong commitment to the work and the mission of the company
- Clear desire to add value and contribute
- Shared urgency to solve the challenges

We followed with a snapshot of the challenges:

- Both teams function as separate teams and separate companies
- Different cultural styles are clashing and eroding trust (formal versus informal, process versus ad hoc, speed versus quality, etc.)
- Want more guidance, communication, and clarity from the CEO
- Roles and responsibilities, handoffs, and work processes are unclear (they know the goal but don't know how to get there together)
- Haven't defined working and cultural norms and expectations

Gordon read the report and called to say, "There are a couple of themes in the challenges that surprised me, but I'm pleased with what you heard were strengths, particularly that shared sense of urgency to solve problems."

He asked a few questions for clarification and was ready to move forward. "So, what's next?" he asked. "Where do we go from here?"

Jane and Peter wanted to lead a team that operated like a team, with the various players working synergistically toward the same goal. We suggested a two-day off-site meeting in which the team members could begin building trust and opening more effective lines of communication. We would use the session to work through the alignment issues, and the team would walk out with a clear plan of action.

Peter and Jane had requested that Gordon kick things off to show he valued this team. They wanted all team members to see that Gordon was committed to supporting the team in resolving whatever issues were holding them back.

"Great," said Gordon. "If we set it up at a hotel in San Francisco, everyone will feel like they're out of the office, and I can come by for at least part of each day."

Two weeks later, men and women from both coasts arrived at a boutique hotel in San Francisco that had the perfect meeting space. With couches and coffee tables, the full team could sit comfortably and talk easily. And the first morning, Gordon kicked it off with a short speech—very short.

Throughout Silicon Valley and beyond, Gordon's reputation rested on the speed with which his mind worked. When people talked about Gordon Street, they remarked on his intelligence, his drive, and his ability to focus on the critical data in a sea of noise. People rarely, if ever, mentioned his social skills. Yet when he stood before his Technology team, he delivered.

"If I had to pick a dozen people who I believed were the top minds in this field, a dozen people who I believed could change the future, those twelve are sitting right here in this room," he said. "I was not wrong when I bet that combining forces would allow us to achieve extraordinary results, and I was not wrong in believing in each one of you."

He looked around the room. "But even I make mistakes," he said, and almost smiled. "And one of them was believing that we would all work perfectly together and that the synergy would happen organically, that we wouldn't have to work at it.

"Innovation seems stifled. We're not moving as quickly as I thought we would. But I know you all have as much passion about our business as I do. And I have full confidence that you can figure this out. I'll leave you to it."

No one moved. And no one knew what to say. Gordon stepped into the silence, thanked everyone for showing up, wished them luck, and, as if he had spent all his social capital for the day, quickly exited the room.

Jane spoke up first. "Well," she said, "what a great reminder as to why we are all here. We're letting the differences between us get in the way of our shared vision."

Peter added, "It underscores what Jane and I both believe: that together we can make this happen. We *have to* make this happen. Jane and I are 100 percent committed to doing whatever it takes to get this solved."

As they turned the session over to us, we asked team members to share their hopes and fears for the future of this team. This gets people talking right away. It allows them to connect on a more personal level, and typically, as happened in this session, people see that they are aligned on what they want and don't want for the team. As we captured the responses, we heard the following:

HOPES
- Getting back to innovation
- Delivering on the promise of our work
- Feeling that I can fully contribute again
- Coming together as one company

FEARS
- We miss this opportunity
- Brought together the best minds in the industry and we can't make it work
- We spend time on team building and nothing changes
- We avoid talking about the real issues
- We'll have to give up what we love about our existing culture

"Looks like all of us—no matter which company we started with—have the same hopes and even the same fears," Jane said. "I'm not the only one who's been hesitant to let go of the culture and our old ways of doing things."

We explained that this was not unusual. Often, with clients who have undergone a merger or an acquisition, we hear from team members who fear that changing the culture will erode their competitive edge. When people have been successful—as both the G Street and MassTech veterans were—they believe that the culture is the key to success. Change it, they think, and risk everything.

The pace of meetings and the way people dress are only the most visible signs of a culture. We asked the G Street team to think deeper about their cultures and the reasons they built the two cultures.

"One of the reasons that we moved so deliberately," Peter said, "is that we believe the work is so important, and we don't want to make any mistake that could shake people's confidence in it."

A few people nodded, and Jamal, a mathematician who was Jane's first hire at G Street, said, "That's funny. When I started at G Street—and correct me if I'm wrong, Jane—I think we decided to move quickly for the same reason. We felt the work was so important that we had to move and make decisions as fast as humanly possible."

The conversation continued, with others adding what they liked about their respective cultures and that they were uncertain how to merge the two without losing what's best in both.

We told them that this was exactly the reason Gordon had brought us all together. We explained that each company had built its culture intentionally and that now the merged team could do the same thing. They'd already seen that they shared hopes and fears and values. Everyone believed in the work and in each other, so for the rest of this retreat, we'd help them use that shared belief to build a new culture that worked for all of them.

We took a short break and waited for everyone to settle back in before we introduced the concept of a Loyalist Team. We walked through the traits and characteristics of the highest-performing teams and then showed the common ways in which teams fail.

When we had explained all four team types, we asked where everyone thought they fit.

"I'd say we're Benign Saboteurs," said an engineer from Boston.

"I agree with her," said another from Palo Alto.

"What?" Jane asked and looked at Peter. "I would have hoped for Situational Loyalist. I don't think any-one is only in it for themselves or doesn't support the team agenda."

Jamal said, "Well, I guess the question is, which team?" He looked at Peter and continued, "I mean, Peter, you're great, but really? You're still drinking from your MassTech travel mug? Even here? Today?"

Peter looked down and sheepishly pushed away the mug sitting on the coffee table. "Yeah, maybe we're more like two teams pretending to be one," he said.

It was an ice-breaking admission. One of the team leaders had acknowledged what everyone instinctively knew but hadn't known how to address. And it gave us momentum going through the rest of the off-site meeting.

We divided the team into smaller groups, gave each one an easel, and asked them to list what's working well and what's not with the present team setup. When we combined the lists, here's what we saw:

WORKING WELL
- Really smart, knowledgeable people
- Passionate
- Like the people I work with
- Exciting and meaningful work

CHALLENGES
- I don't feel as if my voice is heard or appreciated
- Too many priorities, and they are always changing
- Sometimes I feel like we are off and running and I don't know what I'm supposed to be doing
- A lot of the time I don't know what anyone else is working on
- We duplicate efforts too often
- We aren't collaborating well on the highest-impact work

Peter stood up and walked over to the easel. "Wow, seeing this in black and white makes it all clear. We have some real work to do."

He looked at Jane and then turned to the group and asked, "What do you need to see from us that would make a difference?"

Peter barely finished the question before people started shouting answers. It didn't matter whether the home base was Boston or Palo Alto; everyone had something to say. And everyone seemed to speak at once.

"We want you guys to have shared goals and plan together."

"We want you to be co-leaders and not act like divorced parents."

"If we're going to act like a team, we want to see that it's important to you two. We want you to make it a priority."

And when the conversation started losing steam, Jamal said, "Look, I know me. I'm going to fall back into my bad behaviors, so it's up to you two to hold me accountable."

At this point, we jumped in. "That's great. Thanks for your honesty. And what we know about teams is that it's everyone's responsibility, not just the leaders'."

This seemed like a good place to wrap up for the day, so we sent them off to get dinner.

The next day, we divided the room into three groups of four—with representatives of both coasts in each group. And we gave them a simple assignment: talk about a leadership challenge you've been wrestling with and unable to resolve.

Almost immediately, the volume in the room increased. The full G Street tech team was an intense group, and after the raucous last session on the first day, even the Bostonians felt comfortable talking through issues and brainstorming solutions.

After about an hour, when the conversations were winding down, we had the full group reconvene to share what they'd learned. The single biggest revelation for each group was that their colleagues had lots of insight, suggestions, and often, solutions. Each group reported that while they routinely asked questions of their original colleagues, they'd somehow overlooked the fact that an incredible resource was available to them at any time at the end of a phone. They could engage in cross-country problem-solving without going through Peter or Jane.

"I feel like I've been waiting for divine intervention, only to learn that I could call Palo Alto for the answer," said Lauren, a Boston-based biologist.

"You're saying we are heaven-sent?" Jane joked.

The mood in the room lightened, and the two leaders looked relieved to see that the bottleneck they'd been struggling with could give way to something more dynamic. If information flowed from more points to more points, instead of running through the middle, more ideas would be generated and vetted at a greater speed, and more people would be on board.

For the Palo Alto crowd, this felt like a gift: they'd have answers as they needed them. And the Boston crew felt the same way: they'd know the thinking that went into their colleagues' speedy decisions.

To keep the information flowing and to prevent a return to old patterns, we asked each of the G Streeters to identify two or three people in the room they had to get to know better in order to work together better. The team committed to growing relationships by setting up a standing call or adding something into their routine that forced them to stay in close contact.

"And you know," Jane added, "there are airplanes and they go back and forth. If you need to see each other, buy a ticket and meet in person. I'd hate to think three years from now that we missed out on eradicating insidious diseases because we chose to save $500 on airfare."

Everyone smiled, and Peter said, "It's funny and she's right. We have no reason not to get this right. This opportunity—this team of people and this technology—it's not going to come together more than once in a career, more once in a lifetime. We need to own this moment."

From there, everyone admitted what they knew to be true: they'd miss the opportunity if they continued to work the way they'd been working for the past year.

We challenged the group to translate this desire for change into concrete actions. "Okay, what are the first critical steps you need to take?" we asked.

"Can we start by doing a full assessment of what everyone is working on?" Jamal asked. "We don't even know."

Peter nodded and Jane said, "Yep, I agree. That's the first step to breaking down the silos. What's next?"

We helped them consider ways to drive collaboration and what that would look like. Ultimately, the full team decided that they had to be willing to put everything on the table, examine the way they worked together, and consider changing their individual roles and responsibilities and even who reported to whom.

"Shaking up the org chart?" Peter said. "That's exciting. This feels big."

Jane and Peter made it clear that they would make this work a top priority. They agreed to come back to the team with an outline on how to begin tackling this by the end of the following week.

"You guys are really headed in the right direction," we said. "You've made incredible headway. This is a strategic shift that will drive big change, but it's going to take some time. Let's talk about some basic problems that we can solve right now. Who's got something that we can tackle immediately?"

One woman from Boston, who hadn't said much yet, spoke up. "It bugs me when I get into work in the morning and find an email that came in overnight asking me to attend a meeting first thing," she said. "Can we agree not to do that? Can we say no 11:00 p.m. invitations for 9:00 a.m. meetings?"

No one had a problem with that, so other people voiced their requests, which we wrote down:

- Define agendas and hold meetings in which we actually stick to the agendas
- Pick up the phone if you have a problem
- Talk directly to the person who can solve the problem, as opposed to talking to someone else about how frustrated you are

After a while the door opened, and Gordon stepped into the back of the room. Everyone turned, smiled or waved, and got back to shouting out items on their wish lists. The boss looked bemused and took a seat to watch the proceedings.

- Let's acknowledge and celebrate our victories together
- Provide feedback

- Speak up, challenge each other's ideas in real time, and get issues on the table

When the discussion was complete, we noted that everything on their list was a shared responsibility. "Each of you owns every one of these commitments," we said. "In order for you to become a Loyalist Team, every team member has to show up as a Loyalist."

We wrapped up the session by asking each person to share with the group his or her personal commitments to become a Loyalist. When everyone had spoken, the whole room turned to look at Gordon to see how he'd react.

"Wow," he said. "Can I say something? This is a very different room than the one I left yesterday morning. I'm not exactly sure what happened here, but I am delighted with the outcome and blown away by your commitments. This feels like a new beginning, and the beginning of a new team. I think we should celebrate. Drinks upstairs, anyone?"

Three months later, we scheduled a follow-up call with Gordon, who told us to talk to Peter and Jane first and then circle back to him. When we got Jane on the phone, she was bursting with excitement.

"I knew something had changed that night we went for drinks with Gordon," she said. "I could tell by who was hanging out with whom and that no one really noticed or cared when I left. I think Gordon ended up closing down the place with two people from Boston.

"Don't get me wrong," she went on. "It's not all rainbows and unicorns. We had some tense discussions around what to do first, but we hung in there and I think are making real progress. There are times I see us falling back into old behaviors, but the team is doing a pretty good job of calling it and addressing it in the moment. It's often two steps forward. The good news is it is only one step back."

True to form, Peter said he watched and waited for a while after the off-site meeting. He was cautiously optimistic but knew life had changed when one of Jane's direct reports suggested that it made more sense for him to report to Peter instead.

We were excited to hear this. Normally, changes to an organizational chart are mandated by leadership. When a team member requests a change, it shows a significant commitment to and a profound understanding of the needs of the larger team. We told Peter what we thought. "This represents tremendous progress for the team. Changing the org chart is often the toughest part."

"And that was the first domino," he said. "Now, we've realigned the full team. It's no longer organized based on geography alone. It's led to a couple team members relocating. I'm sure our travel budget tripled, but it's worth it."

Gordon had the final word, though, and it was great. "Jane and Peter really stepped up, and productivity is improving," he said. "I'm not worried about missing opportunities with the tech team anymore. My executive leadership team, however, that's another story. Maybe we can schedule a session for them."

THE STRUGGLE TO BUILD LOYALIST TEAMS
IN A VIRTUAL WORLD

Among the forces that push a team to become Benign Saboteurs, mergers and acquisitions lead the list. The challenge of globalization is a close second. As technology and trade agreements allow more companies to compete on a worldwide stage, more people end up working far from corporate headquarters. Companies rely on teams of people in remote offices who mainly communicate with their colleagues by email and text messaging.

Marta Manning ran such a team. As the head of global HR function for Sunlight Telecomm, she supervised people in North America, Europe, Asia, and Australia. For most of her ten years on the job, she focused on overall strategy, executive compensation, board engagement, and running the corporate office while trusting her team to take care of the day-to-day demands in their areas. She liked to say she hired the best and then got out of the way.

And, to be fair, she'd have a hard time getting in their way, if that was her wish. Three of her direct reports were in Atlanta, but the rest lived in Hong Kong, Paris, and Sydney. Marta encouraged each one of them to honor the culture in which they worked and to make decisions to benefit the local team in which they were embedded. If the HR director in Australia devised a talent management plan, great, Marta let her run with it. If her counterpart in Paris designed a training program, that was great too. She could test it, tinker with it, and roll it out across Europe, as long as she kept Marta in the loop. At times, Marta would ask a team member to share a new or exciting idea with his or her HR peers if she thought it would be beneficial elsewhere. And, of course, everyone was responsible for implementing the few global policies that governed performance management and code of conduct.

In 2013, however, Marta called us for a consultation because the mandate was changing. Sunlight's new CEO wanted to run the company more efficiently out of the Atlanta headquarters. An extensive external review had uncovered numerous inefficiencies, duplications of effort, and different standards of work that reduced overall company profitability and called its reputation into question. With some high-profile safety concerns in one region, a public-relations nightmare of an ethics investigation in another, and a new global systems implementation looming, the old local model of control wasn't going to work any longer.

The new CEO wanted to leverage best practices and identify inefficiencies while still delivering the most valuable and necessary services at the local level—and he wanted to start with HR.

"I have six people who report to me, and we're scattered across a fourteen-hour time change," Marta said. "The push to globalize operations will have a big impact on our work and our lives."

As she told us more about her team, Marta painted a picture that looked more like a group of individuals working in tandem than a team working together. Each person had his own agenda, his own priorities and strategies. A few of the more veteran team members also had pet projects that kept them energized.

Each region interacted with the central office team in different ways and at different intervals because how and if they interacted was up to them.

By Marta's estimation, there was no ill will among any of the team members. Mostly, they didn't know one another well enough to like or dislike each other. Occasionally, Marta would request an all-team call, but the logistics were always a challenge—someone would have to be on the call in the middle of the night—so she didn't do it often. Mostly, the team knew each other as names on group emails and only heard from each other when someone hit "Reply all."

"Now, I need everyone to come together and become aligned around the new structure and new approach," Marta said. "And I need it to happen quickly. This globalization initiative is important to our CEO, and my team needs to lead the way."

Marta wanted to continue the conversation with us in person. She needed to be in Colorado Springs for an industry conference the following week, so she arranged to fly in a day early to meet with us in Denver. When we sat down, she told us she planned to bring her entire team to Atlanta for four days. Could we help?

We told Marta that the environment she described is one we see often with teams that are scattered around the world. And the reason is simple. It is easier for all of us to connect with people we see every day. We get to know each other through simple, low-stakes conversations about the newest TV show, traffic on the way to work, or the weather.

For a team that hardly knew each other, an in-person meeting would be the fastest way to bring them into alignment and begin building the relationships they'd need going forward. We agreed to help plan and facilitate the meeting, but we needed more information.

The status quo, Marta said, worked well for her team members. They were happy in their positions and well-liked by the people in the regional offices. Marta's concern wasn't about any one of them—rather she was concerned that together, in the current configuration, they had fallen into a pattern of repeatedly reinventing the wheel instead of calling each other or collaborating.

"All of our regional offices—not just the HR function—are really committed to keeping their local culture," she said. "As a result, one person in Hong Kong might create an entirely new program when a similar one in Paris could be tweaked to work just as well for the Asian offices."

People on her team, Marta said, enjoyed a significant amount of autonomy. They liked running their own show and creating new programs, and she liked that about them. "They're entrepreneurial in spirit, and I don't want to lose that," she said. "And I don't want to lose any of them."

Marta and her team needed to adapt to the new initiative—they had no choice—but we knew that they didn't have to surrender their individual identity or creativity. If they learned to work as a team, individuals who had been running solo would gain the support of colleagues who were facing similar issues, solving similar problems, and grappling with similar ideas. All of them would benefit from sharing expertise and bouncing ideas back and forth. The support would free them to go beyond the day-to-day to tackle bigger issues.

We told Marta about Loyalist Teams and walked her through the four team types. We explained that the highest-performing teams demand the most from their members but also offer the greatest rewards.

To achieve this result, every relationship on her team would have to be Loyalist in nature. And while every person on a Loyalist Team is responsible for her relationships across the team, the leader has to set the bar high. Marta would have to trade in her laissez-faire leadership style, really dig in to understand what her team members were working on and how they were communicating with each other, and then facilitate relationship building whenever connections faltered.

Marta thought a moment. We could almost see the calculations being carried out in her head—adding up hours in the office and on the phone, subtracting moments with her family, estimating the number of flights and days away from home, and settling on what was right for her company and her team.

"What worries me most is that my job is already demanding with my responsibilities to the Board and leading the corporate office," she said. "But I don't have a choice. This has to happen. And I hate to say it, but I think we're a Benign Saboteur Team right now."

We knew that to be true too. As she talked about her team, we had been mentally checking off the traits and characteristics of Benign Saboteurs. And while we generally like to run the Loyalist Team 3D with new clients to gather insights from all stakeholders, we didn't need that data in this case.

For one, we could rule out three of the four team types based on what we already knew. Saboteur Teams require at least one person who is actively disrupting some or all of their teammates, and Sunlight's global HR team didn't cross paths enough for anyone to take on that role.

We ruled out Situational Loyalist and Loyalist Teams for similar reasons. Marta's team didn't have each other's backs, and they couldn't commit to team success—hallmarks of the Loyalist Team types—because there wasn't a clear idea of what either meant. The team members were too far apart and too disconnected to be anything other than Benign Saboteurs.

And, of course, the timeline influenced our decision. The team was assembling in Atlanta in one month, so we opted to limit the number of assessments and get straight to work.

When her whole team arrived in the same room for the first time, *they* needed to get straight to work. We needed to craft an agenda that gave them enough time to discuss both *what* they work on and *how* they would work together. In broad brushstrokes, the meeting would look like this:

Day 1: Discuss Sunlight's overall strategic direction and align HR priorities

Day 2: Create the vision for the HR function and build the HR-specific plan

Day 3: Build the global HR team

Day 4: Move forward through an action plan

We talked through the big picture with Marta in person and then scheduled a few phone calls to finalize details over the next four weeks. And those weeks flew by for all of us.

When we landed in Atlanta, Marta met us at the airport.

"I came to get you myself because I'm so excited about this whole event," she said. "My team is all here. They're all looking forward to working together, and the CEO is so fired up that he keeps talking about using this as a blueprint with other departments."

The next morning, we saw that enthusiasm in action when the CEO addressed the HR team. A charismatic man, he went around the room shaking hands and welcoming each person individually. He talked about Sunlight's proud history and the elation he felt when he took the job. His tone changed, however, and became more serious, when he discussed challenges the company was facing and the ways globalization would help fend off the competition.

"The entire company will be adopting the approach of driving globalization across each function," he said. "And you lucky folks will be first. I'm counting on you to find the smoothest path forward and to show the rest of us the way."

Going a little deeper into the need for globalization, the CEO explained the overall strategic plan. Treating the HR team members as if they were his peers, he showed what he believed were the most likely areas of growth and the company's plan to go after those opportunities. He talked about risk and how the company was prepared for that. And he concluded with praise for the people on the team.

"Hard act to follow," Marta said as he finished. She thanked her boss for kicking off the four-day work session and introduced us to her team.

"These women will lead us through conversations and exercises designed to teach us to work better together," Marta said before telling us about each of the members of her team.

Veronique ran HR for the European division from the office in France. She spoke four languages and was, as you might expect, stylish and a careful observer of details. Wen was the youngest of the bunch. In his early thirties, he had studied in the United States before returning to Hong Kong. And Olivia was the chattiest. An Australian with a gentle laugh, she'd been cracking herself and her teammates up from the moment they entered the room.

Two of the Americans were named Pete. Tall Pete ran Talent Management and the other Pete ran Total Rewards. Lizbeth oversaw Recruiting.

From there, Marta talked through the HR plan and priorities for an hour before opening up the conversation for questions. And there were many.

"I hear what you're saying about globalization, but I don't see how it will change my priorities," Wen said. "Everything I do is so tied to the unique needs of the regional team in Asia."

Veronique nodded as he spoke and added, "I like the idea of working together more, but I don't know what anyone else is working on. I'm not sure how I could be helpful to anyone from where I sit."

We hear similar comments whenever we work with virtual teams. As a general rule, the remote team members are not actively withholding or hoarding information, or otherwise working to sabotage a teammate. Usually, we find that each person focuses on doing the best job they can in their own corner of the world, without looking too far afield. They are teammates in name only who believe they are helping the company by being the best they can be for their region.

With Marta's team, we saw the familiar pattern. They had never been encouraged to reach out to one another. And they had never seen a reason to do it on their own.

We explained that it's difficult for any team to achieve shared goals and desired business results when team members are not clear on what is shared. And they can't have clarity on those goals if they don't talk regularly and intentionally.

"Makes sense," Olivia said. "So what do we do now?"

Always grateful when someone provides the perfect segue, we launched into the next item on our agenda: helping them to list, catalogue, and compare who was working on what, where the lists overlapped, and where they left gaps. We spent all afternoon mapping out the various projects, adding timelines and notes, and looking for patterns. Some of the team were still fairly jetlagged, so once everything was on the board we sent them to an early dinner and went to get one ourselves.

On day two, they started to define their shared vision for the global HR function. Everyone seemed excited about the opportunities, but they had fears and concerns, too. Some worried that they would lose credibility with local leaders who relied on them for quick solutions to local needs. Others worried that they might be forced to roll out a program that was at best irrelevant or at worst insensitive to their local community. The balance of the day was spent decoding the map of current projects and forecasting it into the future. Many of the current initiatives would continue, albeit in different ways, and new initiatives relating to the new strategy would be added. The team would have to step up to make sure globalization could work for both the company and the regional teams. Marta talked about how they could accomplish more by leaning on each other and staying in closer contact.

"I know that at first glance globalization may seem like it's all about loss—loss of autonomy, loss of your local culture, loss of control," she said. "But I'd like for you to think about what we gain too. Right now, we're all freelancing. Everyone in this room has deep-seated expertise that they rarely share. Not because anyone's hoarding but because no one's asking. With globalization, we can leverage our best HR practices and talent and experience to become a team where each one of you is surrounded and supported by HR colleagues who not only know what you do but actually care and can answer questions and troubleshoot issues with you.

"Starting tomorrow, we'll begin to build that team."

By the time we met for the third day, the team members knew each other well. And we had gotten to know each of them too.

When we showed them the dashboard-like model of team types, with Saboteurs on the far left and Loyalists on the far right, they all nodded as if to say, "Go on." We gave a brief description of each team type, handed out the checklist, and told them to mark the boxes that applied to this team.

Veronique was the first to finish. "Oh, no no," she said. "Benign Saboteur sounds so destructive, and yet that's what this adds up to."

The Petes agreed. Lizbeth nodded and said, "It almost sounds like it's sabotage by stupidity or, maybe more accurately, thoughtlessness."

She was right. And, we explained, the way out of any Saboteur situation is by being intentional in your choices. The highest-performing teams make deliberate decisions on how they will work together, share information and communicate. These decisions become the operating norms that Loyalists choose to live by. While some agreements work for most teams, the complete list is individually tailored to meet a team's specific needs.

We asked Marta's team to consider their must-haves and start calling them out. People suggested ideas, tentatively at first, and then with more vigor. We captured each idea on a whiteboard:

- Assume positive intent.
- The work of this team will take priority over other commitments.
- Make sure you understand what you're hearing first before challenging another's ideas.

- Carefully balance the needs of each region with the priorities of the global HR team.
- Actively learn about the different cultures that we support.
- Everyone is accountable for speaking up (and since speaking up to challenge one another is more difficult on the phone, we will ensure that there is time for everyone to voice concerns).

"That's a great start," Marta said. "What's missing?"

Wen shifted in his seat a bit before saying, "I know that the majority of us are in this time zone and that Veronique can catch a morning call here when it's early evening in Paris. That leaves Olivia and me on the late shift. Can we think about that?"

As aspiring Loyalists, the others quickly agreed to share the pain. They would rotate the times of calls so everyone would have the chance to call in at odd hours. They also agreed to schedule in-person meetings every six months in the various offices. The next time, everyone would assemble in Paris. After that, Hong Kong.

"One more thing," Veronique said. "I spend most of my day speaking French and occasionally German. It's difficult to read and respond to English on the fly. Can we agree that we'll distribute anything we have to read well in advance of our meetings?"

We added that to the board and double-checked that the list was now complete. We knew that these norms would make an enormous difference if everyone bought into and obeyed them. We also knew that if we had ended the week right there, we could have called it a success. At that point, the team knew each other, knew what everyone was working on, understood and had aligned on priorities, and agreed to operating norms. And we still had the afternoon and the next morning ahead of us.

Oftentimes, on team-building retreats, team members are told to pair up and interview one another. The individuals get to know each other; they learn about each other's family, hobbies, and work history. Maybe they're asked to introduce their new friend to the group as an icebreaker activity. Other times, on other retreats, teams play golf together or do a ropes course, hoping that spending time together outside the office will dramatically change behaviors inside the office. Sometimes that works, but it's not the most certain or effective way to move a team forward. Watching someone shank a drive or listening to them reminisce about college days can be fun, but neither experience necessarily prepares two people to work together.

Before we let everyone go to lunch, we asked that they think about the most pressing item on their own agenda and identify the person they need to work with to get it done. "Come back ready to sit down with that person and dig into it," Marta said. "Have a good lunch. Our new way of being a team starts when you return."

From our discussions with Marta and observing the team over the first three days, we had a sense of who would need to work with whom, and they returned in the pairs we expected. Wen paired up with Tall Pete. Veronique worked with the other Pete. And Lizbeth and Olivia sat down together.

We'd prepared worksheets to guide them through the conversations. The first page was a list of questions:

- What are the key priorities and goals in your role?
- What's most stressful for you in your current role?
- What are your biggest challenges?
- What does success look like in your current role?
- In our shared work, what does success look like to you?
- What's at stake for you personally in this shared work?

Once each pair had discussed and answered the questions, we asked them to fill in a diagram to help visualize their discoveries.

The worksheets also included exercises to help them identify and discuss their own work styles and

Your purpose, my purpose, our shared purpose

YOU · · · · US · · · · ME · · · ·

preferences, as well as any barriers they might see in working together. And on the final page, we asked them to agree to work plans. Each person needed to write down the actions he or she would take next and describe how they would work together to create joint work plans.

Lizbeth and Olivia immediately decided to go for a walk outdoors and talk through their choices. Wen and Tall Pete sat down at a table and went at the task old school with pens and paper. The other Pete and Veronique pulled out a laptop and took notes electronically.

After two hours we told them time was up, and all of them begged for more. "Just twenty more minutes," Wen said.

"How about half an hour?" Olivia said.

We weren't surprised that they asked for more time. Whenever we do this exercise, people deeply engage. When given the opportunity to build an authentic connection, they dive in. More than an exercise, their conversations and connections become real and meaningful. People are usually grateful to feel that they are part of something bigger than themselves. Often, clients report that they're inspired by seeing their work in the context of advancing the goals of the whole organization.

"We'll give you another fifteen minutes," we said. "We need time to debrief."

When the team members finished the task, they were excited and eager to follow through and work together.

Tall Pete may have summed it up best. "The way I could be a better HR professional is not just by doing my job better, but by being a better member of this team."

Lizbeth looked at Olivia and said, "We were both surprised to learn we had a lot more in common than we thought we would. It was really clear what our shared purpose could be."

We suggested that, as homework, they vow to run through the same worksheets with another member of the team within the next six months.

At the end of that third day, Marta handed out Braves baseball caps to everyone and announced plans to go to the game that evening. The next day would be the last, and it would be the easiest, only a half day long. We wanted them to run through timelines, goals, assignments, and the very practical matter of next steps.

Once all of that was locked down and everyone knew what was ahead of them, we asked the team members to tell us how they were feeling.

Other Pete said, "I'm exhausted and proud of what we've accomplished."

Marta added, "I feel like this is the beginning of something really important for us. And for Sunlight as a whole. Now we really can be role models."

Sunlight's HR team understood the concepts and owned all the tools needed to become Loyalists. If they carried on and committed to being intentional in their choices, they would become the team that they all desired.

And we know that's a big "if." Often teams come together for a few days, listen to their leaders and fa-cilitators, and fail to follow through. People come to meetings, nod and smile, maybe even take notes, and then return home to do exactly what they had always done. We knew there was a chance of that happening here but felt success was the more likely outcome. We sincerely hoped the team would make strides and learn to be Loyalists. As we said goodbye, we promised Marta that we would continue to be a resource for her as she and the Sunlight team forged this new path.

LEAVING BENIGN SABOTEUR HABITS BEHIND AND BECOMING A REAL TEAM

Benign Saboteur Teams maintain the status quo and are stagnant and slow to change. These teams commonly exhibit wasted potential and lost opportunity.

You know you're on a Benign Saboteur Team when:

- There's a "keep your head down" mentality; you do your work and don't rock the boat

- You just want to be left alone

- Your team meetings are dull—typically just going around the horn without real collaboration or conflict

- There's a "stay in your lane" understanding that keeps you from giving feedback or challenging others—even if it's critical

- You don't feel safe showing uncertainty or lack of confidence

- You withhold giving feedback to members of your team; it's not a risk worth taking

- It feels more like a group of people who happen to work together rather than a real team

Benign Saboteur Teams can't deliver extraordinary results because:

- Artificial harmony keeps the real issues from being discussed

- There's little to no risk-taking or innovation

- Personal and team development are non-existent

- The focus is on personal goals over team or organizational results

- The team's true potential is unmet

If you lead a Benign Saboteur Team . . .

1. Take control.
The good news is your team isn't a Saboteur Team. The bad news is that without action, it could become one. By accepting the status quo, you risk going in the wrong direction.

2. **Involve the team.**

On a Benign Saboteur Team, people do not see themselves as a team. It's our job to change that by involving the team in setting a vision for change. Work with the team to define your shared purpose and establish a plan for working better together.

3. **Set priorities and shared goals.**

Bring the team together to agree on priorities—agree on what work you will and won't do. Create shared goals and success measures. Agree on ownership and accountability for delivery. Craft a set of nonnegotiable operating norms to reinforce the new culture of involvement.

4. **Invest in building relationships.**

Benign Saboteur Teams typically lack strong connections between teammates. Reinforce the importance of the team interactions and collaboration. Make time for team members to get to know each other at a deeper level.

5. **Drive accountability.**

To maintain momentum, check in frequently with the team on its progress. Talk about what the team is doing well and where more work is needed. Address setbacks head-on.

6. **For remote teams, go the extra mile.**

If you can afford to bring the team together, do it. Choose to communicate by video instead of audio whenever possible, and cycle through time zones when scheduling your meetings. Also, invest in cross-cultural training to make sure team members understand each other's cultural nuances.

If you are a member of a Benign Saboteur Team...

1. **Seek ways to engage and collaborate with teammates.**
   Members of Benign Saboteur Teams tend to stay in their own silos and only engage with a few select colleagues. Take a sledgehammer to the silos and look for opportunities to collaborate with or acknowledge the success of others. Don't wait to be invited in.

2. **Ask for and offer help.**
   You can set a powerful example for change when you reach out to others and ask for or offer help. When you are struggling, don't just double down on your efforts. Ask your colleagues. And when help is offered, graciously accept it. When someone on the team is struggling, reach out and offer help and support.

3. **Step up.**
   Bring your "best self" to work every day and lead by example. Don't be passive about making the team better. Benign Saboteur Teams need powerful leadership—not just from the top. And they are hungry for a deeper level of teamwork and better results.

4. **Communicate.**
   If you're in a remote office, pick up the phone instead of relying on email. Set up a video

conference whenever you can and schedule time to get to know one another personally. Build the relationships that you'd have in the office and that will allow you to support one another.

Benign Saboteur Teams can leave the people on them feeling isolated in their workplace, whether the team is in one location or spread out over many. Some people find comfort in the isolation because there's no need to worry about anyone but themselves and no need to look beyond the narrow confines of their own job description. The comfort, however, comes at a high cost. Benign Saboteur Teams also cause stagnation. When everyone keeps their head down, it's nearly impossible to continually get better, drive change, and accomplish team goals or organizational goals. And individuals suffer too.

People on Benign Saboteur Teams aren't challenged in a way that leads to personal growth and development. And when leaders are looking for someone to promote, they rarely look to those who keep their head down and play it safe all the time.

Still, the outlook is far from bleak. When team leaders and members start to understand and practice the behaviors of a Loyalist Team, they can improve their status pretty rapidly. We've seen teams that seemed locked into Benign Saboteur habits become Situational Loyalists within a few months, and then team members find that both their individual and team goals are more attainable.

5 SITUATIONAL LOYALIST TEAMS: IF IT AIN'T BROKE . . .

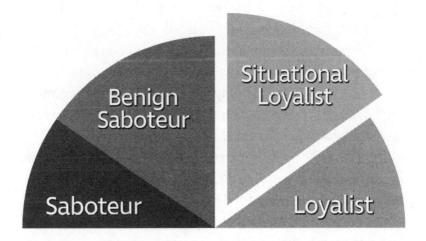

WHEN THE LOYALTY COMES WITH CONDITIONS

Kathryn often wondered if she did her best thinking driving on Detroit's Lodge Freeway to and from ATR's global headquarters. The head of North American Sales for the auto parts giant, she had so many big ideas on that road that she'd gotten into the habit of telling her car to call her office so she could leave herself a voice mail.

One evening on her way home, she thought back to the meeting with Carl when he told her about the problems he saw with the team. As the newest member of her team, he had taken a brave step by coming to see her and asking why decisions were routinely made outside the team meetings. Carl wondered why the team bothered to meet at all if they never discussed anything of substance in the meetings.

Less than a mile into her commute, Kathryn called her office and said, "Carl brought a new set of eyes and saw something none of us could see. How did I insert myself in the middle of every decision, and how do I change it? See if Tony has suggestions."

Having left the voice mail, Kathryn could try to let it go for the evening.

The following morning, she listened to her messages, jotted down the three ideas she'd sent herself, and walked down the hall to Tony's office. Officially a member of the HR Department, Tony was the North American Sales Team HR Business Partner, and while he wasn't responsible for selling car parts like the rest of the team, he was as much a member of Kathryn's team as any of the regional sales managers.

"I wondered if you could help me think through something?" she started and gave Tony the highlights of her conversation with Carl. She told him how decisions were mostly made in one-on-one conversations and that the team used their time together to go around the horn, with each person giving their status update. Tony agreed that the staff meetings rarely seemed to include any give-and-take and instead sounded like a series of brief monologues.

"Your team moves and makes decisions so quickly," Tony said. "I didn't realize that the team was calling you at home evenings and weekends to get the go-ahead. And I think you're right—it's a great team, and although they seem to work pretty well together, there is certainly room for them to collaborate more. I'm just not sure they know another way."

We had worked with Tony at another organization earlier in his career. He told Kathryn about us and suggested setting up a call so that she could tell us what was going on and see if we could offer any insight. Kathryn was eager to explore her options, and we could see why.

On our first phone call, we introduced ourselves and talked about the way we work. We asked questions about the team members and the challenges they were facing.

Katherine told us how much she trusted and respected every one of them. She talked about individual strengths and how proud she was of the milestones they were reaching.

"Honestly, if not for two things, we could continue indefinitely as we are," she said. "We do amazing work."

Those "two things," however, kept Kathryn up at night. It didn't matter how much she tried to capture issues on her voicemail and leave them behind for the night. Between the Carl conversation and a new competitor in the market, she was exhausting herself with thinking and rethinking and overthinking.

Late at night and again on her morning jogs, she'd think of Carl and roll through the same questions. "Why are our meetings so polite? I'm not afraid to mix it up. How come my team and I don't dig into the real issues?" Even in the office, between phone calls with her team, Kathryn would wonder if she couldn't be a more effective leader.

The second issue was rattling the entire auto parts industry. ATR had been a market leader since long before Kathryn joined the company. Recently, that lead looked like it might be in jeopardy. A smaller start-up had the agility to move quickly and the audacity to come after ATR's talent. Almost every week, Kathryn heard of another case of the new company trying to hire ATR veterans and profit from the relationships they'd built.

"They have the potential to cut into our market share," Kathryn said. "To maintain our command of the marketplace, we have to grow sales by double digits this year—and I'm nervous."

We asked if she thought the two issues were related. "Even though one challenge—the team meetings—is internal, and the new competitor is external, how do you think they impact each other?"

Kathryn understood that the two were related. She just wasn't sure how they connected or how to work on both at once.

We talked about how the internal workings of a team drive external performance. If the team members did not work well together, they'd be limited in their ability to meet an external challenge.

Tony had been listening to the conversation and jumped in to add context. "The whole company is concerned about the new competitor," he said. "There's lots of pressure on Sales."

All the more reason to make sure the team was in alignment. We shared what we learned from our research: that the highest-performing teams are created intentionally and that with the right actions and focus, every team has the capacity to become one of them. We explained that nothing would change without bringing the team together and making time to discuss the opportunities.

Kathryn and Tony each wanted to understand the time and financial commitment involved. And Kathryn, results-oriented as always, had one more line of questioning. "How quickly," she asked, "can we expect to see results?"

The speed of progress depends on how deeply a team digs in and how forcefully they commit to each other and to doing the work it takes to build a high-performance team. With the right commitments and investment of time and energy, the shift comes quickly for our clients. Usually, they see a dramatic change within six months, if they do the work.

"If that's the deciding factor," Kathryn said, "we should be fast. No one works harder than my folks. Really, I can't tell you how motivated they are. But they travel a lot, and we're all meeting in Chicago next month for a Sales kickoff. I can't schedule another meeting on top of that."

A better option, we suggested, would be to have her team fly in one day early for the sales kickoff so that we could work with them then.

"Perfect," Tony said. "That should be easy to coordinate."

Kathryn sent emails introducing us to each of the team members, explaining what we were hoping to accomplish and how we would work together. She requested that each person make himself or herself available for an interview.

A long-time lieutenant of Kathryn's was the first to respond. Tomasz Budzynski (Bud) joined the company the same month as Kathryn. The two learned the ropes together and always counted on each other for support. When Kathryn was promoted to become his boss, Bud was neither surprised nor envious.

"She's so smart," he told us. "It's like her brain works faster. Getting to work for her has been great for me. I couldn't call our old boss to work through decisions or on weekends, but Kathryn's always available to me. And I know she's always there for everyone else. That's how our team works."

We interviewed Justine next. A sharp Texan who knew every player in her territory, Justine owned the state like she was some kind of Lone Star royalty. When we talked to her, we learned that, like her peers, she felt a strong bond to the boss.

"Kathryn's amazing," Justine said. "And the team works really well together. No offense to y'all, but do we really need to do this team-building business? Do we have time? Excuse my language, but we now have a serious competitor, and I have a big-ass quota. I need to focus on sales."

That same day, in a separate interview, we heard an opposing point of view. Carl was the newest member of the team and his estimation of Kathryn was consistent with that of his teammates. He thought she was a talented sales professional, one to watch in the auto industry, and a great leader—no disparity there. But when we talked about taking time to work on team dynamics, he was ready to clear his calendar before we even asked.

"How many days do you need?" he asked. "I'm grateful for the opportunity to work for ATR. And my colleagues are great, but I still think about my old job. We had our issues, but when it came to meetings, we could really put our heads together and break something down. Sometimes the conversations were heated, but at the end of them, we all knew we'd come to a great decision together.

"I miss that," he said. "At first, you know, I felt like I was being left out of the loop here. But over time I started to think there is no loop."

We asked Carl about the relationships on the team, and he hesitated. "Well," he said, "I like everyone. I think they're good at what they do, but I don't know much about their work. Our relationships are not that deep."

With Kathryn, Carl said he liked and trusted her and would even say their connection was solid.

"I call her when I need to, but I wonder—and I hate to say this, but I wonder if she's the reason I don't feel that connected to the others," he said. "Do you know that she was a point guard in college? She likes to run the play and be in the middle of things."

As we interviewed team members, we also collected data through the Loyalist Team 3D. We asked Kathryn's team and key stakeholders on the executive team to complete the questionnaire. From their responses, we deciphered how the team's estimation of its strengths stacked up against the expectations of executives. They had concerns about the North American Sales Team, scoring the team lower than the team scored themselves and including comments like, "You are bleeding talent at a time when our growth goals are steep."

We compared the overall quantitative data from the assessment to our database and determined that Kathryn and her team were in fact a Situational Loyalist Team.

On these teams, there are deep pockets of trust and a shared sense of purpose. Situational Loyalist Teams are intent on increasing performance but may still deliver inconsistent and uncoordinated efforts, especially when leadership or the external landscape changes. They tend to struggle when a new competitor shows up, as ATR was discovering.

We analyzed the quantitative data and used the qualitative data from the interviews to add texture to the report that we shared with Kathryn and Tony. Once they had the chance to read it, we met with them in person.

The headlines on the report started with the positives:

- People are passionate about ATR and its products.
- There is a high level of trust and little politics.
- They have a lot of respect for each other's capability and expertise.
- They are subject matter experts with deep sales experience.
- Team members have a deep loyalty to Kathryn as a leader and view her as critical to the team's success.

We followed with the challenges:

- The team gets along but members don't challenge or debate one another.
- Team members are reluctant to call each other out.
- The team doesn't solve problems together; instead, they go to Kathryn.
- Team members' primary focus is their regional responsibilities.
- The relationships are positive, but team members operate independently. There's no awareness of interdependence.
- Team members want Kathryn to get out of the weeds and focus more on the longer-term strategy and vision.
- Lack of coordinated planning and goal setting creates duplication and inefficiency.
- Company executives fear that the sales team is not holding on to top performers.

Tony was initially surprised. He had assumed that to function as well as Kathryn's team did, they'd have a strong, if not perfect, team dynamic. As he spent more time with the report, though, he reconsidered team meetings and conversations he'd had with Kathryn. Tony realized that the report gave voice to a secret that had been hidden in plain sight.

"Kathryn, this is great," he said. "I can see how all roads go through you. And I think if we can change this, move you out of the middle, and free you up to do more strategic thinking, the benefits will be huge. You can really step up and contribute at the executive level. And your team can develop their skills and advance their careers."

A lot of the work we do is teaching leaders how to lead at the right level. Even the most accomplished execs sometimes get distracted by their team and end up doing the team's work instead of the leadership-level work they need to be doing. We've seen this in all industries and nonprofit organizations. When the leader understands how to lead at the right level and begins to reallocate her time and attention, the team tends to move up quickly.

Kathryn nodded. She had been trying to help her team by answering questions and making decisions, but she hadn't realized that her efforts, while well-intended, might be holding them back.

TEAM ACCOUNTABILITY MODEL

Traditional team accountability flows from the team leader to each team member. The team leader plays a central role in driving accountability for results and behavior.

Loyalist team accountability flows between team members, as well as the team leader, who hold each other accountable for results and behavior.

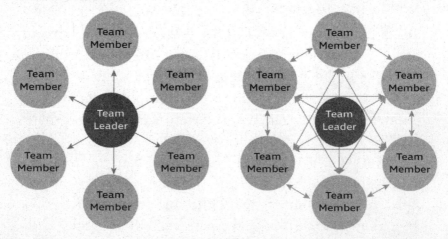

"I think this hub-and-spoke setup is the way it's always been with this team, and it's the way I work with my boss," she said. "I love my boss, but to tell the truth, I often think if he left the rest of us would be screwed. I wonder if that's what my team thinks."

"Yes" was the short answer. In our interviews several members told us variations of the same thing.

We walked Tony and Kathryn through those and other comments from the interviews and the Loyalist Team 3D. Both were eager to get going, and the sales kickoff was just weeks away.

The day before the sales force landed at O'Hare Airport, Kathryn greeted her team in a library-like meeting room in a Chicago hotel. Five regional sales leads, Kathryn, and Tony all settled easily into the club chairs and couches. Looking around the room at the bookshelves filled with leather-bound volumes, Bud said, "Seems like we should be drinking single malts and smoking cigars."

"Maybe we'll get to the Scotch at the end of the session," Kathryn said and smiled. "For now, we have work to do. We have a great foundation of trust, and I'm incredibly proud of what we've accomplished. That said, I know there are things I can do differently and ways we can collaborate more effectively.

"And it's critical that we take this on now. If all we had to do was grow by 2 percent, we could keep going the way we have been," she said, looking around the room for agreement. "Or if we were the kind of people who could settle for good, we could just continue on. But why settle for good when we can reach over and grab great?"

Big smiles spread around the room. Kathryn wasn't the only one with a deep-seated competitive streak.

"As we go forward," she said, "I want us to be open to exploring new ideas of ways we might work together. I want us to look carefully at how we collaborate, to consider what we absolutely do not want to change and what we're willing to let go of. For me personally, I see this as a turning point in my own leadership. I've been doing the same things in the same ways for a long time now. I know I've helped this team succeed, but I think I'm also holding the team and myself back. I'm ready to take a hard look in the mirror."

Kathryn took a seat and gave us the floor to introduce the Loyalist Team concept. We showed them the model that depicts the four team types, with the least productive on the far left. As we explained the habits of a Saboteur Team, people winced.

"People survive on teams like that?" Justine asked. "Sounds horrible."

As we described the traits and characteristics of the middle team types, we saw recognition, as if everyone in the room understood how those teams could happen. But we really saw heads nodding in agreement when we talked about the Loyalist Teams, the highest performers that we've studied.

"Yeah, that's us," Justine said. "Absolutely, we have each others' backs all the time. And for Kathryn, most of us would lie down in traffic if she needed us to."

Kathryn smiled and shook her head. She knew that was part of the problem. The sharp and extremely capable members of her team were also extremely comfortable taking direction from her. Too comfortable.

Without intending to, she had enabled them to become overly reliant on her. She'd inadvertently created a system in which they waited for her signals to accelerate, decelerate, or switch lanes.

We had to break it to them gently. As much as they carried good feelings for one another, they were not Loyalists. Justine screwed up her face as if we had just told her there was no Santa Claus. Bud looked as if he wasn't quite sure. And Carl looked excited.

"We have something to aim for," he said. "Isn't that the goal here, to be a Loyalist Team? I'm all for that."

And that was exactly why Kathryn had convened this meeting and set aside the time and resources to improve internal dynamics and external results.

Situational Loyalists are the most common team type we work with. Part of that is self-selection. These are the teams that are not complacent. Leaders and members of these teams know they're doing well and recognize that they could be better still.

In some ways, they're the most fun teams we work with because they're close to reaching their peak potential. But in many cases they can be some of the most challenging because they are good teams that are very comfortable with the status quo. Members of the team care about one another but have no forum for healthy conflict. As a group, they don't wrestle frequently enough with tough issues. Instead, they create workarounds, which in this case was going to Kathryn. The alternative route works—the individual gets the answer he or she needs—but because the whole group wasn't involved in the deliberation, other members of the group don't benefit. Mostly, they don't even know what happened, what was decided, or the reasons. They may run into the same issue and have to start at square one.

With Kathryn's team, we could see it clearly. She and the regional sales leaders who reported to her had not considered their options or deliberately decided to organize themselves into a hub-and-spoke system. It just happened over time and became self-reinforcing. One regional leader would run into a roadblock and mention it to Kathryn, and she'd remove the block. The next time he faced a similar block, he knew the solution: ask the boss. It would never occur to him to turn to another regional lead for advice or support.

The hub-and-spoke system also clouds over an important reality. As we see in many organizations, Kathryn's sales leaders served on at least two teams. Each was a member of her team, the North American Sales leadership team, as well as their regional team. One is horizontal: the sales team is responsible for a function across an organization. And the other is vertical: the Western regional team is responsible for a number of functions, top to bottom—supply chain, marketing, customer service, sales, technology, and others—in the Western region.

Typically, one team takes an elevated role and demands first allegiance, and the second team takes the back seat.

What we saw with Kathryn's team was that all members prioritized their time and attention as if the regional team was their primary responsibility and checking in with the sales team was an afterthought. This worked well enough for a while—because they were skilled professionals and Kathryn filled the gaps between them—but when a new competitor changed the external landscape, the team needed to change the internal dynamic. They needed to pull together as a Loyalist Team. Each member needed to commit to the same level of engagement with Sales that each had with his or her regional team. They needed to get creative, collaborate, and share resources across the organization to make sure they hit ATR's ambitious sales goals.

To become Loyalists on their horizontal team, each person needed to share in the responsibilities of planning for and achieving the North American sales results. Each Sales leader must contribute to the conversations about North American sales. The lens on the business needed to be wider than it was on their regional or vertical teams. The conversation, debates, and trade-offs should not be how each person will achieve individual goals but instead how they will deliver on the North American sales goal collectively.

As the newest member of the group, Carl saw this pretty quickly. "At my old company, we all built our sales plans together," he said. "When I got here, I was surprised that everyone developed their plans on their own."

Bud shrugged and said, "Well, we're all traveling so much, it just seemed easier and faster to do it alone. And honestly, I didn't see how we could collaborate on that. My clients are so different from yours, and my regional challenges are unique."

He was right. On the ground level, their work was different. But at a higher level, they faced similar challenges.

"Yeah, it's true," Kathryn said. "You each have regional responsibilities that can look different, but we are all facing an increased sales quota. Look, Bud, I need you on board here. We're not going to solve this if we don't come together as one team. "

Kathryn also addressed the need to keep the new competitor from poaching their best people. So far, she said, it looked like a regional issue, but if left unchecked it was only a matter of time until the competitor would come after ATR staff everywhere.

"Yeah, those jokers keep coming after my people," Justine said. "I've lost two and had to fight like heck to retain two more that they wanted. It's a nightmare."

Bud looked concerned. The competitor had been poking around in the Midwest, but Bud put an end to that in a hurry.

"After they came after one of my guys, I instituted a retention program and went full throttle on it," Bud said. "Haven't lost a guy since."

Justine shot Kathryn a look that needed no translation.

"Oh shit, I'm sorry," Kathryn said. "I thought I told everyone what Bud was up to. My mistake."

We couldn't have scripted a better explanation for the value of cross-team communication and team-wide collaboration. By focusing on his regional team role, Bud had solved a local problem. But if he'd been thinking of his sales team role, he would have shared his solution—or, more likely, he would have engaged his teammates in creating it. He didn't even know the other regions had the same issues.

After lunch, we reconvened in the library-like room and were pleased to see that people had reorganized themselves and chose to sit in different chairs, between different colleagues. Kathryn had moved from a seat closest to the door to a seat on a couch on the right side. Two team members plunked down beside the boss as if she were just another teammate.

"This morning's session really helped me see how each of you identifies more closely with your region than with this group," Kathryn said. "You know, it's more 'I'm the Western region lead' than 'I'm a member of the North American Sales Team.'

"And I'm sure I've fostered that to some extent by talking to each of you individually about your regions," she said. "Let's all commit that this team is our priority, and let's think about what synergy exists here."

To discover the actions that would lead to synergy, we asked them to define the role of this team and its purpose. With a few iterations, they agreed upon a straightforward description:

"This team is charged with creating the overarching direction for all ATR Sales in North America, and we are responsible for ensuring that the regional sales plans in each region come together to serve the entire organization. We are responsible for making sure the sum of the parts is greater than the whole."

When we asked them to brainstorm actions they could take in support of that mission, they immediately discussed meeting more often and with greater intention. They quickly killed the status update meeting, where each one gave a quick synopsis and only Kathryn listened. The others often used the time to check their email or plan what they were going to say when it was their turn to speak.

The regional sales leads discussed and committed to meeting in person for two days, three times a year, to discuss big-picture ideas, share best practices, and write and review their plans together. And for her part, Kathryn promised to direct them to each other more often.

"If something like the retention issue were to come up now, I'd tell Justine to check in with Bud," Kathryn said. "I'll keep pushing you to call each other until you do it on your own. These are exactly the types of issues we should be spending our time on."

The team covered a lot of ground in one day by focusing on how the team could work together better. With teams like this, where there is a certain amount of trust, we end the day by asking each person to seek feedback from her peers. We wouldn't do this with Saboteur or Benign Saboteur Teams because the relationships aren't strong enough and people don't feel safe enough to give or receive honest feedback. On a Situational Loyalist Team, however, the exercise can help team members learn to put hard conversations on the table, to strengthen the relationships with peers, and to see where they can learn from one another.

Finally, we asked each of them to fill out a one-page feedback sheet on each other:

- What do you value most about this person?
- What could this person do to be more effective?

- What could this person do to better support the effectiveness and alignment of the team?
- What commitment will you make to this person to develop and maintain a healthy Loyalist relationship?

We challenged them to be candid and courageous in their feedback. They spent some time preparing and getting ready to share. Loyalist Teams practice giving feedback. By doing that here, in a safe space, this team would start to build muscle memory around this practice.

After a short break, we reconvened the group for the final session of the day. We asked them to give the pages they'd completed on each teammate to that person. Then we gave them fifteen minutes to read their colleagues' comments and formulate a summary-review from them.

When they'd organized their thoughts, we had each person share what they learned.

"What I learned," Carl started, "is that you appreciate my industry knowledge and that I am bringing new ideas and insights to the team. I also heard that you'd like me to be more proactive in sharing what I see, especially when I think there's a better way to do something.

"What I'm realizing in reading these comments is that even though I've been here six months, you don't feel like you know me that well," Carl said. "And you aren't sure I'm fully committed to this company. I'm still talking about my old company too much, and I have to stop that. What I need from all of you is this: please call me and give me a heads-up when something's coming down the road that you all see every year. There's a good chance I won't know to expect it, so please don't be shy about getting on the phone."

A few of the teammates apologized for not doing that already. They had figured Carl was too busy. They assumed he knew what was coming and didn't want to seem patronizing.

"Oh no, don't worry about it," Carl said. "I'd rather be over-prepared than caught off guard."

Each member went around the room sharing insights and requests. And the response to each was similar. People were happy to be invited into each other's orbits. They hadn't thought about asking one another's help with troubleshooting or problem-solving.

When it was Kathryn's turn, she committed to staying out of the weeds by facilitating more conversations between team members. "I won't exactly hang up on you if you call," she said. "But I'm going to remember that when you do call, it doesn't mean I have to offer a solution. I trust all of you, and I know that among the group, you have all the tools to sort things out in a way that promotes sales on the continent, not just in one region or another. I'm also committing to bringing the team together more frequently and with more intention."

As we were wrapping up the session, a final question came up.

"Are you telling me that being a Loyalist means I have to unconditionally support someone who's not pulling their weight?" Justine asked.

Kathryn jumped in. "That's not us. Everyone on this team is pulling their weight and then some. We don't even need to talk about it."

"Hang on," we said. "That may be true on this team, but that's still a great question. We know being a Loyalist Team is not a substitute for having the right talent in the right positions with the right skills. Everyone on a Loyalist Team must be able to perform and do their job well. However, if you're not the boss, you don't have the authority to fire or reassign anyone. What is not okay is being that person's Saboteur."

We went on to say that being a Loyalist requires that everyone remain a Loyalist at all times. If one member of the team sees someone struggling, it's that person's responsibility to initiate an honest conversation, provide support and assistance, and even go to the manager if the team's success is in jeopardy.

"I sure hope that if I were in over my head, or if any one of you saw me heading for a cliff, that you would be honest with me and talk to me about it," Bud said.

There was general agreement in the room. And as we left, we felt confident the team was on the right track.

Six months later, it was Tony who called us. He described the changes in the team's dynamic and how that allowed Kathryn to really shine with her peers and the executive team.

"It's really amazing," Tony said. "The team has been working together to put the retention plan in place, and we haven't lost a single person since that meeting. The dynamic feels stronger. They are starting to problem-solve, and the meetings have taken on a different tone. In many ways, Kathryn's stepping back, and there's more space for her to lead at the executive level."

The team, he told us, was on target for their sales quotas.

"Kathryn and I are even talking about how we could change their incentive structure. The regional sales leaders said, 'Since teamwork is so valuable, we want to be rewarded for doing well as a team.' Isn't that great?"

Yes, it is great. And ATR's North American Sales Team was well on its way to joining the ranks of the Loyalist Teams.

LOYALTY TO THE MISSION IS ONLY ONE PIECE OF THE HIGH-PERFORMANCE PUZZLE

Situational Loyalist Teams, like the one at ATR, are often humming along and doing good work. Often, the work seems good enough. Not great. Not summiting Everest, but moving steadily toward the goal. We see Situational Loyalists in sales teams that cover great stretches of territory, and we see them among executive and entry-level teams that work together in corporate offices. We also see them in nonprofit organizations. It's easy to assume that the men and women on mission-driven teams support each other as Loyalists because they share a vision of how to make the world a better place. Unfortunately, committing to the organization's goals doesn't always ensure that the individuals commit to each other, or that they know how to be Loyalists.

Theo Robbins ran the Kelly Family Foundation, a nonprofit that was dedicated to improving education. The Foundation awarded $20 million annually to community organizations working in three distinct areas: early childhood education, teacher development, and postsecondary preparedness.

A one-time junior high school teacher, Theo still dressed like one: khakis, brown shoes, plaid button-down shirts. A childhood friend of the Kelly kids, he had joined the Foundation a dozen years earlier and was promoted to executive director five years before he called us.

"We lost a major donor," Theo said. "And we're struggling."

We told him fundraising wasn't in our wheelhouse, but he quickly cut us off. "No," he said, "It's not about fundraising. One of my board members, who knows you, told me to call you because we're struggling to make decisions in the wake of the funding cuts. She thought it was a team alignment issue and that you could help."

The Foundation employed thirty people. The leadership team included Theo and six others: three program directors (one in each of the Foundation's areas of interest), an attorney, the head of fundraising and development, and the director of marketing and communications.

One of the Foundation's largest donors had decided to change course and direct his giving to other organizations. "He still cares about education," Theo said, "but it's not his top priority anymore, so we lost about 15 percent of our operating budget."

The donor had made the announcement a year in advance of the change, so Theo and his team had known for some time that as they planned future giving they'd have to make some hard choices. And hard choices made them uncomfortable.

When the team started discussing budget cuts, Theo told us, members immediately and almost reflexively reached for ways to avoid making decisions. They considered using a formula to cut the budget—say, a 15 percent cut across the board—which seemed fair and equitable. As an unspoken bonus, no one would have to denounce anyone else's program, and everyone could duck responsibility.

As they talked about the ramifications, though, they decided that forcing every program to suffer equally didn't feel equal or intelligent. The team then swung to the other extreme. Instead of spreading the pain across all their programs, they could isolate it by cutting one entire area of work and sparing the other two. No one wanted to, but theoretically the team could eliminate early childhood education and increase involvement in the other areas. Or cut teacher development in favor of preschool and postsecondary readiness. Or cut postsecondary efforts and bolster the others. None of these wholesale cuts seemed like good options.

Finally, they knew they would have to consider reducing overhead costs at the Foundation.

Theo hoped his staff could approach the problem more thoughtfully and make cuts in a strategic and surgical way.

"We've been kicking this around for months, and we're running out of time," he said. "We have a meeting next week, and I was hoping you could come and guide us to resolution."

We told him we could come and observe his team's interactions and listen to what people said and what they didn't say. We thought it would be important to see his team in action before providing guidance on where decision-making might be stuck. Then we could share the habits and patterns we saw and make suggestions from there.

"Can't you just tell us the answer?" he said, and then sighed. "Okay, let's plan on that."

To prepare for the meeting, we asked a few more questions. Theo told us that each member was deeply committed to improving education. They were all passionate about their work, and the three program directors had built strong relationships with the organizations they funded. Each had research and solid arguments to support why investment in their area would result in the greatest educational outcomes for students.

"Each one of them cares so deeply that they've all come to me to lobby for their fundees," Theo said. "Serena works with early childhood, and she was in tears in my office. She didn't want to let people down, and she couldn't see why preschoolers didn't automatically jump to the front of the line over teachers and high school grads."

As Theo talked about the situation, he sounded stressed. Serena wasn't the only one tugging on his heartstrings. Soledad ran the teacher development programs and, like Theo, was a former teacher. "You know how hard it can be in the classroom," she said. "If the teacher is lost, the kids have no shot at success."

Even Charlie, a retired executive working on his second career, had come to plead his case. "You know, Theo," he'd said, "a college degree is like a high school diploma used to be. Doesn't matter if they get through high school if they don't go to and graduate from college. We've seen the statistics: graduation rates for low-income high school and college students are abysmal."

Theo knew all of this. He knew Charlie was right, just as he knew Serena and Soledad were. All three funding buckets were meaningful to Theo personally, to the Kelly family, and to the families in the community they served. "I'm really at a loss," Theo told us. "I hope you see something at our meeting that breaks this logjam."

The following week, we went to the Kelly Family Foundation's offices and found Theo at his desk. "Glad to see you," he said, and walked us down the hall to the conference room where the leadership team was assembling.

Theo introduced us as experts in teamwork. "We make a great team," he said to his staff. "We definitely work well together, but we've come to a sticking point, and I hope a fresh set of eyes can help us see a way through it. They are here today to observe and get to know us."

We introduced ourselves and explained that we wanted to see them in action before providing recommendations. We said that mostly we were there to observe, but we might ask a question or two to gain clarity as the conversation went along.

We took seats at the back of the room and let them get to work. As expected, Serena, Soledad, and Charlie all made impassioned pleas for fully funding their projects. They talked about the organizations they funded and the kids who benefited from each. All three of them said that if the Kelly Foundation pulled support, there was no one to fill the gap. These programs would shrink or disappear, leaving struggling kids to struggle more.

Each person argued for his or her area, and no one disagreed.

Soledad said, "I see all of your points. I believe in all of our programs. This feels like trying to cut out one body part to save another. I respect all of you and the incredible work you do. This just sucks."

Heads nodded, and no one changed their mind. No one saw an alternative. Everyone seemed dejected, overwhelmed, and stuck.

The conversation went around and around again. Slowly, we glimpsed the alliances that were starting to form and how cautiously individuals tiptoed up to what they feared might upset another member of the team. The director of marketing suggested that funders preferred to support little kids. "I'm not the expert that you all are in the benefits of each program, but I just want to mention that it's easier to raise money for preschool programs than the others," she said.

Soledad and Charlie locked eyes immediately, and when there was a break in the conversation Soledad said, "Serena, I know you do really good work and you're incredibly passionate about it, but, you know, early childhood is sort of the odd one out. Teacher development and postsecondary preparedness go hand in hand, and in these areas, our programs build on one another."

We thought we were seeing the beginnings of real discussion, but almost as quickly as these conflicting perspectives arose, they were gone. No one responded. No one probed. No one asked questions. The prospect of heated debate was too uncomfortable.

Situational Loyalist Teams like this one haven't honed the practice of making tough decisions. Team members prioritize being nice to one another over anything else. In an effort to avoid conflict, they discount their own assertions by saying things like, "I'm sure you know better than I do, but . . ." and they compromise before they even engage. Often, there's an unspoken assumption that disagreement is inappropriate.

Theo tried to push the group to consider what could be cut. Instead of arguing in favor of what each person wanted to protect, he encouraged them to suggest the programs they could let go. When he said this, we saw everyone's eyes drop to the table.

Eventually, Charlie said, "Theo, you decide. We'll all do whatever you want. We can't make this decision. We all trust you."

Theo shrugged, looked at his watch, and suggested they take an hour for lunch.

The leadership team filtered out of the room, but we stayed with Theo. We waited for him to close the door before telling him what we knew about teams. We walked him quickly through the four team types and explained that even in this brief encounter, we saw the telltale signs of a Situational Loyalist Team: the commitment to organizational goals, the desire to keep things moving, and the pockets of trust that were leading to alignment.

We also saw a reluctance, if not complete refusal, to put the tough issues on the table and engage in honest debate. As soon as anyone inched toward conflict, visible discomfort and desire to stick with the status quo overtook them, as if they needed to reassure one another. Theo's team wanted him to make the tough call so they didn't have to. Of course, he could make the decision, but it would be a disservice to his team and to the kids they were all committed to helping. The three program directors had the most detailed knowledge of programs they funded and their impact. Theo had a ten-thousand-foot view, but his team members were on the ground.

On a Loyalist Team, individuals benefit from each other's critical thinking. On a team where members are committed to each other's success, a vigorous debate works to sharpen everyone's thinking. Loyalist Team members take adversarial positions as a show of respect—they want to test each other, and they trust that they can.

"My team has the best intentions," Theo said. "They just don't see challenging one another as a way to show that."

The problem was a little deeper. We explained that individuals on Situational Loyalist Teams don't have the same level of trust as Loyalist Teams, not across all members of the team. It's not that they mistrust each other as much as they aren't certain what will happen if they charge into debate. Maybe someone will get hurt, or maybe someone will become angry; no one knows the outcome, so they hold back in an attempt to protect one another or themselves.

When Situational Loyalist Teams come to a fork in the road, as the Kelly Foundation team had, they can use the experience to strengthen their relationships and become a Loyalist Team. Or they can take the path of least resistance. They can act intentionally and voice their concerns, or they can fall backward into less productive patterns. If not tended to, informal alliances can harden into competing factions. The pockets of trust can dissolve into conditional arrangements: I'll trust you if you do this for me or if you don't do that for her.

"Great," Theo said with exasperation. "That all makes sense, but what do I do? I mean, what do I do right now, when they're all looking to me to decide?"

We suggested he start the afternoon by telling his team what he saw. He knew they cared for each other and cared about the programs and that something was holding them back.

"You could just ask them what it is," we suggested. "They know the conversation is stuck. It might be interesting to hear what they think is the cause."

We also suggested Theo tell them what he knew: that they were strong enough as a team and that their relationships were solid enough to withstand disagreements. They could disagree about policy without making it personal. And they would benefit from healthy debate.

Finally, we suggested that he extract himself from the situation.

"What do you mean? Tell them to figure it out and get back to me?" he asked.

"Yes."

If what Theo had said about his team was true—that they had deep knowledge of their programs and were sufficiently committed to the mission and to each other—then yes, they could find their way to a solution without his help.

And it might be the only way for them to do it.

"I feel a little guilty abandoning them," he said, "but if you think it's the right thing to do, I'll try it."

We did, so we wished him luck and left him to it.

We heard from him the next day, and he sounded optimistic.

"It seemed to work," he said. "When I asked them what they thought was holding us back, I was surprised by their answers. I thought they didn't want to lose their turf. I thought they were skeptical of each other's abilities or commitment. It turned out they didn't want to step on each other's toes. They were worried about being disrespectful of each other's hard work and the importance of their programs. And they felt so beholden to each of their funding recipients, letting them down with less funding felt like a betrayal and a breach of their values and integrity."

Theo had given his team a deadline and went back to his office to get work done. He was still sitting at his desk when Soledad stuck her head in at 6:00. She told him they hadn't reached a decision yet but felt confident that they would. She asked if the team could regularly schedule meetings without Theo.

"At first, I was a little hurt," he confided to us.

We assured him that this was a good sign and that he should be proud of his team and proud of his leadership. It's a sign of growth when team members feel they can step up and own decisions as a group without the boss. And in this case, they thought they'd have a solution they all could support by the end of the week.

"Soledad said that once they got into it, they really let go and even brainstormed ways to combine efforts in existing programs," Theo said. "They started looking for ways to make any cuts less painful."

Without the boss in the room, the team pulled out research they'd done a year earlier that compared the effectiveness of the Foundation's various programs. The team ranked the programs and looked for ways to restructure or streamline them.

"It made me stop and consider the way I've enabled program-specific thinking," Theo said. "I probably need to let go more. I clearly underestimated them.

"If they can take on more of this tough decision-making," he added, "it frees me up to do more fundraising, so maybe they won't have to. That's my hope, anyway."

Ours too.

GOING FROM GOOD TO GREAT: MOVING FROM SITUATIONAL LOYALIST TO LOYALIST

Situational Loyalist Teams feel positive and productive, so quite often there's no urgency to improve. They leave value on the table by settling for "good enough."

You know you're on a Situational Loyalist Team when:

- It's a good team but could be better

- You have strong and trusting relationships with several team members, but not all of them

- You are willing to help and collaborate when asked

- You're prepared to meet others halfway

- The team relies too heavily on the leader for decision-making, conflict resolution, and feedback

- Peer-to-peer accountability and healthy conflict happen in pockets

- The fear of discomfort or harming a relationship keeps you from having the hard conversations

- When the going gets tough, you can't necessarily count on your teammates to have your back

Situational Loyalist Teams limit value because:

- They settle for "good enough" instead of pushing for greatness

- When things go wrong, the team hesitates instead of digging deep and pulling through

- An overreliance on the leader disempowers the team

- Not all team members are fully committed to all other team members, at least not every day

- Feedback is often too "safe," and the toughest issues aren't discussed

If you lead a Situational Loyalist Team . . .

1. **Drive shared accountability.**
   Odds are, you're a good leader, and the team tends to overrely on you. Reflect on your part: Are you managing conflict for them? Are you working at the right level and delegating appropriately? Are you making too many decisions for the team? Establish shared goals that require deep collaboration.

2. **Drive peer-to-peer coaching and feedback.**
   The next step for your team is getting comfortable being uncomfortable by giving—and receiving—feedback. Be willing to push through the discomfort in pursuit of greatness. Lead by being vulnerable and relentlessly seeking—and giving—feedback.

3. **Don't settle.**
   Don't let your well-intentioned team deteriorate or become content. If you don't see overt signs of trouble, it's easy to settle. Set a vision for greatness, and talk to the team about its progress early and often. Move the bar higher and give the team members confidence that they can go further.

If you are a member of a Situational Loyalist Team . . .

1. **Model peer accountability.**
   Confront your team's accountability challenges. When you see positive or negative team behavior, call it out. Appropriately and

respectfully identify others' behavior that is inconsistent with the team norms. Take ownership when you have failed to live up to them as well.

2. **Own tough conversations.**
Be the one to talk about the elephant in the room. Everyone else sees it. The conversation will move quickly once it starts. Most team members want to have real conversations about the real challenges.

3. **Ask for and provide feedback.**
Giving and receiving candid feedback is hard, especially to peers. But Loyalists take this on because they're committed to each other's growth. Without an explicit agreement, it's daunting to step in and provide feedback to peers. Be the first to ask for feedback, and when preparing to give feedback ask permission and ensure your intention is to help and support your colleague.

4. **Help your teammates succeed.**
Commit to your teammates' success as you commit to your own.

5. **Build a Loyalist relationship with every team member.**
A team is only as strong as its weakest link. Prioritize the relationships that need the most work. Start by being a Loyalist yourself.

Working with Situational Loyalist Teams can be both exciting and exhausting. These teams have so many effective habits and good tendencies, but at the same time they can be resistant to change because everything feels pretty good as it is. Team members like and respect one another, they're proud of the work they do, and they feel like this is as good as it gets. That feeling, however, is deceptive.

If your team is a Situational Loyalist Team, congratulations. You're doing many things right. But there's still another gear and still more you can accomplish. Don't settle when you can move forward and become a Loyalist Team.

6   LOYALIST TEAMS

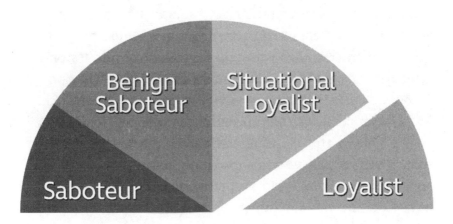

Ian Campbell took the call from his daughter, as he always did, and she immediately handed the phone to his granddaughter.

"Grandpa, Grandpa, you should have been there!" the seven-year-old screamed. "I skied a black diamond today. First time! It was awesome."

Ian listened to her tell the tale, told her he was proud of her, and promised that he'd be there the next time. Then he hung up and looked around his office. It was a nice place, comfortable enough and convenient enough in the Denver Tech Center, but he was sitting in the office while the people he loved most were chugging along I-25 after a bluebird day on the slopes.

At sixty-two, Ian could still ski bumps. As CEO, however, he had few opportunities to do so, and even fewer on weekdays that coincided with the grandkids' spring break.

Ian pictured his daughter driving the carload of kids. And he pictured the conference room full of executives waiting for him down the hall.

Ian knew his team was tough and smart and talented. He remembered how inspired he was at the retreat they had in the fall. Each person had taken an active role, challenged old conventions, listened to each other—even the hardest feedback. And it didn't stop after the retreat. He knew his team had been firing on all cylinders ever since.

"It's time," he said to no one but himself.

Ian joined the meeting and was pleased to see his team had started without him. Together, they were considering options and working through the thorny issues on the table. They'd be fine without him. Ian considered his decision for the rest of the day but was pretty certain he was ready to retire. At home that night, he asked his wife if she was ready. They'd been talking about his retirement for months, and now the conversation took on a new urgency. They talked long into the night and agreed to give themselves the weekend to decide. By midday Sunday, they knew. Ian wrote an email to Susan Timms, his Chief Human Resources Officer, asking her to meet in the morning. He hit the send button and felt a mix of anticipation and fear. What was next for his team?

In the morning, Ian delivered the news with little preamble. Susan listened intently, and while she was sad and surprised, she was also a professional. She knew a smooth transition required careful planning, so she swung into action and started firing off questions: "What's the timeline?" "Have you scheduled time with the Board?" "Who else needs to know? And when?"

Ian said he'd like to stay through the end of the year, so a new CEO would have to be selected and ready to roll in nine months.

"I can take care of the logistics and make sure everything's in place on our end," Susan said. "Do you feel you need help managing the team dynamic as we go through this?"

Ian nodded and suggested Susan call us right then.

"Hi," she said. "You're on speakerphone, and I'm sitting here with Ian."

We had worked with him early in his tenure at the company. At the time, the entire domestic apparel industry was just starting to show signs of life after a twenty-year drought. In its fourth decade, Torreys Clothing, a privately held company, was one of the few firms that could even remember the boom times. And as a new CEO, Ian had understood that immense planning, tight forecasting, and aggressive scheduling were required to make the model work. He knew then that he needed a high-performance team to hold it together.

Now, as a more experienced chief executive, Ian's concern was holding the team together.

"We have a Loyalist Team, no question," he said. "And I want to make sure it stays a Loyalist Team as we transition to the next CEO."

Ian had two internal candidates and believed both were ready for a top job.

"They are key members of this team, and either one of them would be a great leader," Ian said. "And the team as a whole is exceptional, but I've been down this road before. Remember?"

Yes, we did. Ian had been Executive Vice President of Sales and one of three internal candidates vying to become CEO. The three had been colleagues who suddenly felt as if they were pitted against one another. The competition dragged on for a year. Everyone inside Torreys, it seemed, had a horse in the race. People were gossiping and sucking up to their favorite candidate, or worse, trying to interfere with the ones they didn't like.

When Ian was named CEO, the two other candidates left the company abruptly, and the executives who stayed were exhausted by the drama.

"I don't want to live through that again," Ian said. "And I won't put my team through it. I can't. I care about them too much, and we can't afford the distraction this change might cause."

All too often, we see internal competition over succession planning, and it can damage a business in just the way that Ian had experienced. We told Ian that retaining both candidates might not be possible. If both are ready for the top slot, they would both likely seek it out, either at Torreys or somewhere else. But, we assured him, a repeat scenario of the drama could absolutely be avoided.

The leadership team under the previous CEO was not a Loyalist Team. The members of that team did not have the tools or habits to efficiently navigate big changes—whether those changes were in the marketplace or within their ranks.

Ian and his crew, however, had done the heavy lifting to become a Loyalist Team. And those teams are the only ones that can consistently thrive through change. Because of the strength of the intrateam relationships and the universal commitment to candor, Loyalist Teams can avoid the hidden agendas, gossip, and speculation that lead to infighting.

Ian trusted his team and hoped they could stay focused while his successor was chosen, but he was apprehensive. And he thought it would be helpful to have an outside set of eyes on the process. We agreed to meet with him and Susan in person the following week.

When we arrived, Susan greeted us in the reception area and brought us to Ian's office. It was 9:00 a.m., and Ian was ready to dive in. He had a fresh pot of coffee brewing. His sleeves were rolled up, and he had the succession plan and timeline spread out on the table.

"First off, great to see you all," Ian said. "And second, I have good news already. I talked to the Board Chair and the Board agrees that we don't have to do an external search for my replacement. We have two great candidates in-house."

"What do you think?" he asked, pointing to the timeline he and Susan had drafted. "I have another call with our Board Chair on Friday and plan on talking to Brian Childers, our COO, and Helen Rosen, head of Sales, next week. I figure they should each know about the other, and they can keep it to themselves until we're ready to announce the choice to the full team."

We asked Ian to update us on the complete team, describe how it had changed since we last worked with them, and explain how all the pieces now fit together. When we talked through the entire team, we all agreed that no one would be surprised to learn who the candidates were. Torreys' Chief Legal Counsel had already made it clear that she didn't want the job, the head of Technology wasn't qualified or interested, and the same was true for the head of Creative.

"I recognize that the two candidates are the obvious choices," Ian said. "It's just that I don't want anyone else to feel they have to pick sides. Brian and Helen have unique relationships with each member of the team, and the relationships are what make us work. They're the reason we can stay agile in this industry. My fear is that announcing my retirement before we have a successor will mess up the balance."

We understood Ian's concern. Still, we felt that asking the two candidates to keep a secret from the rest of the team in the long term was a mistake. If they were the only ones who knew Ian's plans, they'd have to rein in their comments in meetings or make choices that they couldn't explain. It would put them under additional stress that might affect their ability to seize the opportunity at hand. And Ian was adamant that he wanted them both to be in the best position to show their strengths to the Board.

We asked about the team's operating norms, and Ian was quick to pull them up on his screen.

- I will grant trust and assume positive intent
- I will subordinate personal and functional agendas for the larger company agenda
- I am as committed to your success as I am to my own
- I will talk to you, not about you
- We will talk about the toughest issues openly and candidly

"Shoot, you're right," Ian said. "I can't tell Brian and Helen that I'm retiring, they're candidates, and they have to keep it a secret. We have built a solid culture of trust, and if I were to ask them to keep this a secret,

I wouldn't feel I was being fully transparent. I don't know how that would work."

We asked him to think about the alternative. What would happen if he granted trust and gave his team two important pieces of information at once? What if he told them that he was retiring *and* either Brian or Helen would take the reins? It's a lot for any team to absorb, and yet we believed his team could handle it. We reiterated with Ian that trust is the cornerstone of every Loyalist Team.

In our work with Situational Loyalist and Loyalist Teams, we've seen teams use outside threats such as a new competitor or a change in the marketplace to pull together and become stronger. Was it possible for a Loyalist Team to use an internal change in the same way?

We asked Ian to consider the possibility that by going through this together, his team could preserve all he'd built at Torreys *and* become a more efficient, higher-performing team in the end.

"Now that we're talking about it, I don't see a better alternative," he said. "We're going to have to try."

The following week, he scheduled one-on-one meetings with every team member to share his plans. Two weeks later, once they had some time to process the news, we followed up with each of them to gauge their reactions.

Before we started our meetings, Ian shared with us that several team members were excited for him but were also sad. They liked working for him and felt his retirement would be a personal loss. Still, they were pleased that the search for a replacement was limited to two people they knew and liked.

Our interviews confirmed what Ian told us and added another dimension: anxiety. Even though the two candidates were known quantities, the future looked uncertain.

When we spoke to Peggy Goodwin, who ran the Creative team, she said she respected both Brian and Helen. "I have high regard for both of them," she said, "but Ian's been such an incredible leader. He's my mentor, and I've learned so much from him. I rely on him, and I don't know that I'm going to have that with any other CEO."

Manuel Sanchez, the head of Technology, was equally sorry about Ian retiring. "He's a tough act to follow," Manuel said. "I think Helen's probably closer to ready. I'm not sure Brian is strategic enough. I can't picture Torreys under Brian's leadership."

When we interviewed Helen, she was thoughtful and humble but still agreed with Manny. "I was hoping I would be the one to get the job," she said. "I really think I'm better qualified, so this is going to be hard. No slight to Brian—he's fantastic—but I don't know if I'd stay if he got it. I'm ready for CEO. I know it is my next move."

Brian had a different take. He was excited about the opportunity and grateful to be considered.

"Everything that's happened while I've been here," he said, "everything—like when we transferred our production from a 500,000-square-foot facility offshore to a series of smaller facilities in the US, or when we refocused our design from winter sports activewear to fitness—all of it has been an opportunity to learn and grow. If Ian wants to take the next six months working to develop both me and Helen, I'm all for it. There's nothing but upside for me and the company."

Once we completed the interviews and organized our thoughts about them, we checked back with Ian. He was grateful to hear everyone's commitment to one another and to the company. He said he was cautiously optimistic that the team could handle the transition without losing a step in the marketplace or their focus on the business.

"How about Brian and Helen, though?" Ian asked. "I want to make sure they're each in the best position to go after this opportunity while still doing what we need them to do every day."

Over the next six months, the Board would be looking to see which of the two candidates was better equipped to succeed. Board members knew that Brian had the skills to run the day-to-day operations, and they knew Helen could deliver results based on the continual growth in sales. Still, there were plenty of unknowns for each of them.

As COO, Brian tended to think more tactically than strategically. He needed to put out fires and pull the levers right now, not five years into the future. And he had limited exposure to the Board. As CEO, he'd need to keep the big picture in mind all the time and show the confidence, decisiveness, and visionary thinking demanded at that level. He would need to demonstrate these qualities to the Board, the industry at large, and all the employees.

With Helen, questions arose around her financial acumen and understanding of Operations. As head of Sales, she didn't need to know every last detail of how products were created, what vendors demanded, or why distribution worked the way it did.

There was also the question of who would replace her. Helen had led the Sales team for six years, and Ian wasn't convinced that her successor was ready to step up and lead the team.

Our conversations with Ian and Susan convinced all of us that Brian and Helen would benefit from coaching as they worked through this process. All too often the request for coaching comes when there is a crisis, a performance challenge, or a deficit. We know the most effective coaching happens during times of transition when the stakes are high, the goal is clear, and there is significant opportunity ahead. We appreciated Ian's foresight. Ian also knew he needed help with the team as a whole. He wanted to make sure the rest of the team received support through the transition.

"We have a great set of operating norms, as you've seen," Ian said. "And I think it might be helpful to refresh them. To pull the team together just for a half day or something, to see if we need new agreements and to anticipate in advance some of the challenges that might arise during the transition. What do you think?"

We agreed that getting ahead of this would benefit the team. And creating a system to guide the transition to ensure success would allow everyone to feel connected and stay focused on the business throughout the process. We selected a date and started preparing for it.

Two weeks later, early one morning, we met Ian outside Torreys' conference room. He looked uncharacteristically nervous.

"I have mixed feelings about this," he said, opening the door for us. "This is hitting me harder than I thought it would."

Inside the room, the full team sat around the large table looking as abnormally subdued as Ian looked wired. After a quick chorus of "Good mornings," the room fell back to silence.

Ian looked at each member of his team one by one. "This is tough for me," he acknowledged. "I'm proud of this team and this company. We've achieved great success and avoided all the potholes and speed bumps that keep tripping up our competitors. We're where we are because we operate with openness, candor, and loyalty. And we're not changing any of that.

"Still," he said, "I have some war wounds from the last CEO transition. Some of you were here last time, and you may remember that it was a struggle that affected me personally and our business for several years. My goal for this morning is for us to talk about how we are going to manage through this transition and all be on the same page."

Around the table, people looked concerned.

We started the session with a temperature check. "You've had two weeks to process the news. What is top of mind for each of you right now?"

One by one, the executives shared the sentiments we'd heard in our interviews: their sadness over losing Ian, their hope that the team can continue on as Loyalists, and their support for the two candidates. A number expressed their natural concerns about this being the end of an era and how important Ian had been in their own professional and personal growth and development.

Helen went deeper and addressed one potential problem.

"I'm not worried about anyone in this room," she said. "My concern is how word will travel throughout the rest of the company. In the absence of knowledge, people tend to spend hours and hours speculating, playing 'What if?' and saying, 'You know what I heard?' 'You know what I think?' How do we avoid that?"

"Let's come back to that," we said. "Let's stay focused on this team a bit longer."

After a moment's silence, Manny spoke up. "I trust you guys, but I've been down this road before. I remember how painful it was when Ian was competing for CEO. We have to do a better job than we did last time."

"The good news is that you've put in the hard miles to build strong relationships that can sustain you through this transition," we said. "However, you will need to keep on it. This is going to test you in new ways."

Ian nodded. "This is going to be hard for me, too. And it's on us to hold each other accountable. At this point, only the Board and the seven of us know my plans."

"Right," Brian said. "What are the plans for us communicating this to our teams?"

Ian looked at us and quickly looked back at Brian. "I know six months is a long time, but we intend to keep it under wraps until we can announce my retirement and my successor simultaneously in September. I'll step down at the end of the year, letting you or Helen take up the reigns in January."

Brian and Helen turned to look at each other as if the gravity of this situation had just landed. Helen smiled and nodded. And Brian did the same. "Okay, we're all in this together," he said. "What's our play here?"

At this point, Ian asked us to facilitate the discussion around operating norms. We posted their current set of norms on the wall and said what they all knew to be true: their norms had served them well. And in light of the new challenges, it was a good time to reconsider them and add to them if necessary. We asked the team what other commitments would help them through the transition.

"I think it's important that we all reaffirm our support for everyone on this team, including Brian and Helen equally," said Manny. Others agreed and added ideas until the final list looked like this:

- I will actively demonstrate my support of my colleagues and this leadership team.
- I will not allow others to speak negatively about a colleague.
- I will not allow or encourage speculation.

After they reviewed the proposed additions, they realized how powerful the original norms were and that the only thing that might sink the team would be allowing themselves to be a party to speculation. The most important norm was the commitment to talk about the toughest issues openly and candidly. The team signed off on the new norms and, ready to get back to work, started packing up to return to their offices.

We sat down to debrief with Ian.

"I think that went pretty well," Ian said. "What do you all think?"

We told him that we thought the team was in good shape and went back through the norms to make sure Ian felt they were complete. We said we'd check in with him periodically and set a date for a more formal check-in in six months, just before the full staff announcement. We left Torreys' offices that day feeling fairly confident that they'd have a smooth transition.

Over the next few months, we received calls from various team members. Even Susan called us.

"I feel like I'm the HR professional so I should be above this, but I'm struggling with what this change will mean for me," she said.

Peggy, the head of Creative, called a week later with a similar concern. "I find it really challenging to work with both Helen and Brian as if nothing has changed," she said. "As if nothing's about to change. One of them will be my boss."

We talked each caller through his or her concerns. We helped each one to stay engaged in the work and aware of the operating norms they all agreed to.

As a team, they were doing really well. They were continuing to support one another and keeping the transition confidential. Everything was going according to plan, until suddenly something outside the team's control forced them to change the plan.

The 9-1-1 call came in August, one month shy of the planned reveal.

"I'm really angry," Ian said, "and there's no one to scream at. A Board member inadvertently let it slip to the Controller. And instead of coming to me or going to the CFO, the Controller turned to his colleagues and sent the rumor mill into full gear."

We quickly scheduled a meeting with Ian and Susan to learn more and discuss the options. Ian and Susan both were crestfallen because everything had been going so well. The executive team had been holding to their operating norms: supporting one another, avoiding speculation, and keeping the whole thing confidential.

"If we ask the team to still pretend it's confidential, we're setting them up for failure," Susan said. "It'd be a charade."

Ian agreed and added that the team—especially Helen and Brian—were already keeping a lot of balls in the air. Tossing one more at them didn't seem fair.

"They're both doing so well," Ian said. "With Brian, it's like we took the lid off. We never asked him to really be a strategic thinker before, but man, that might have been a mistake. He's an incredibly thoughtful guy who's able to see seven jumps down the road."

The Board, too, Ian said, was impressed with Brian. He presented and answered questions in a way that gave Board members a lot of confidence in him.

We asked about Helen, and Ian said that she was also taking the development work really seriously. "She's made major strides in demonstrating her understanding of the company's finances and manufac-turing processes," Ian said. "I'm still wondering if her successor is really ready to step into her role. I'm realiz-ing Helen hasn't done enough to develop the leaders on her team. And that's a crucial part of leadership too—building capacity and grooming the people around you to do more."

And this sent us back to the topic at hand. How should Helen, Brian, and the others talk to their direct reports who have now heard the news from others? The Board still needed time to decide who would become CEO, so they couldn't just jump to the finish line and announce Ian's retirement and his replacement. Not yet.

But now that the cat was out of the bag, they couldn't avoid or obfuscate. It'd be impossible to say, "No, no, nothing to see here," right up until the Board made a company-wide announcement saying the exact opposite.

Ultimately, there was only one answer for this team in this situation. And that was for each member to tell his employees that this transition had started and where things stood today.

"Just pull back the curtains and tell them every-thing?" Susan asked. "Including that we're considering Brian and Helen?"

Absolutely. By narrowing the field to internal can-didates, Ian and the Board showed they had confidence in the team they'd assembled. They had confidence in the path the company was on. In selecting either Brian or Helen, the Board could maintain continuity, keep the team strategically aligned, and avoid disruption. For employees, it would be welcome news.

For a company that wanted to build a Loyalist culture, this was an opportunity to demonstrate what that culture looked like. We advised Ian to share what they knew now—that he'd step down in January and either Brian or Helen would succeed him—and promise to share the decision once it had been made.

Ian agreed and said that once the Board sent out the communication he would hold a webcast to answer questions that came up. He also asked us to be available to help the leadership team if they needed it. As it turned out, they didn't. After Ian talked them through the decision, Susan gave them talking points. And that was enough.

We met with Ian for coffee a month into his retirement. He reflected on how the transition had gone.

"I can't begin to tell you how great this team is," he started, before we'd even said hello. "Brian and Helen made the choice really hard, but in the end Brian rose above. And Helen was very disappointed but so gracious about it."

Shortly after Torreys announced Brian's appointment, Helen was offered the top job at another company. An upscale retail chain that had approached her years earlier about heading their sales team approached her again as soon as they heard about the decision at Torreys. They had talked with her about the chief executive position. It was a smaller company with a strong reputation that was looking to grow its footprint. After a quick interview process, they had offered Helen the job.

"Helen told me she was ready for the challenge and was going to accept the offer," Ian said. "Before I could even respond, she told me how grateful she was to me for the opportunities she had had here at Torreys and how without them she would never have been ready to be CEO."

Helen was so committed to her colleagues and to Brian in particular that she offered to stay for a few months to get her replacement sorted out and to support Brian in his new role.

"Can you believe that?" Ian asked. "It's tough to see Helen leave, but how great is that? It's been a helluva journey."

Brian waited a few weeks after Ian left before he moved into the big office. And even then, he was slow to add artifacts of his own life. Photos of his kids came first. A few weeks later, two plants appeared on the windowsill. And by the time we saw him nine months later, he'd added a stunning photo of Torreys Peak.

"My wife shot that," he said. "When I got this job, we hiked to the summit to celebrate."

And the excitement hadn't worn off. Brian felt he had the best team in the business and the best product in the marketplace. And for a man who liked to test himself, he saw no shortage of challenges and opportunities ahead.

"Things are going great," he said, "but I'm new in this role and we have two new people. In some ways we're a whole new team. I'd like to make sure we're headed in the right direction, that I'm not missing anything.

"Could you do a wellness checkup at our next offsite?" he asked. "I'm thinking it could be like taking the kids to the pediatrician before school starts. Nothing serious, just tap the knees, take the temperature, and tell us if there's anything we need to keep an eye on."

The executive team had a two-day retreat on the calendar. Brian invited us to attend part of it so we could observe and give the group feedback, in real time, on whether they were living up to their own lofty standards.

It wasn't a tough decision. We'd traveled so much of the journey with this team that we felt like part of it. We were committed to their success, so of course we'd be there. We were looking forward to seeing old friends and meeting the new additions.

Victoria was the new head of Operations. She'd been promoted almost immediately after Brian became CEO. She'd been his right hand when he ran Ops and stepped into his shoes so smoothly it was as if they were made for her. The rest of the executives felt confident that she was on the job and supported her as she grew comfortable in it.

Replacing Helen had taken longer, much longer than Brian had hoped. He'd spoken to several candidates who were technically proficient and had the right résumés. They even had the right answers in early interviews. Subsequent conversations, however, left Brian and the rest of the team feeling uneasy, as if something was missing.

The gap was always on the culture side. Candidates knew the industry, had led effective sales forces, and were hungry to grow a business, but each fell short when the conversation turned to their leadership and teamwork beliefs. From subtle clues, the Torreys team sensed the person was too ego driven, too selfish, or too flippant about "that HR stuff." When Brian described the importance he placed on teamwork, leadership, and living the values, another two candidates dropped out by politely declining to continue in the process.

Each time, it was the right decision. In our practice, we've seen clients hire a candidate who had the right background and experience only to find out later that they didn't fit culturally or that their values differed. In cases like these, the majority of executives fail.

"Lauren was the sixth person we seriously considered, and it felt like she was one of us," Brian said. "Susan, Manny, and I met with her at one point, and I think it was Manny who told her that we can be ruthlessly honest about business challenges and personal feedback. She didn't exactly say, 'Bring it,' but she didn't shrink from it either. She talked about her past successes and failures with equal humility, and she spoke eagerly about what she learned from each. It was clear she thrived in collaborative, team-based organizations, and she questioned us about the culture as much as we challenged her."

Brian offered Lauren the position in June, and she started six weeks later. By the sound of it, she hit the ground running. She'd met with her colleagues on the executive team, brought her sales force together for a few days of intense kickoff work, and analyzed Torreys' competitors—all before Labor Day.

Lauren and Brian had a standing meeting on Tuesday mornings, and after the long weekend, Lauren bounded into his office like she was bringing a gift she couldn't wait to unwrap. She walked him through her research and explained where it was pointing. Torreys had an opportunity to expand its market. If the company added a lower-priced line of apparel, she argued, it could appeal to people who weren't familiar with the current brand.

"She was so fired up that I hated to slow her down," Brian said. "But we've been through so much in the last year that I thought it would be a tough conversation with the rest of the team. I told her as much but also said that it would be a valuable conversation. I suggested she pull together her research and introduce the idea at our off-site."

Brian told us a bit more about the retreat—what was on the schedule, what he hoped to accomplish, and the location. He'd booked an old hunting lodge near Rocky Mountain National Park, just ninety minutes from Denver, where we could easily go for a couple days.

When we arrived, the full team was in place and looking like a reunion of staff from a summer camp, or maybe a boarding school. Everyone at Torreys wore Torreys clothing almost all the time. It could be a jacket from five years ago, a sweater from last year, or a prototype from next year's line. Since Peggy had been head of Creative for a dozen years, the whole collection—and in this case, everyone in the room—showcased her taste and sensibilities.

We said hello to our old friends and introduced ourselves to Lauren and Victoria. When everyone had taken a seat, Brian got the ball rolling.

"I asked our friends from Trispective to join us for what I'm calling a wellness checkup," he said. "Aside from our business goals, which are ambitious, we also set our sights on how we want to do teamwork. And the standards on that front are equally ambitious, so I invited them to attend and tell us whether we're hitting the mark. Any questions?"

There were none, so the executives plunged into the business at hand. Brian talked about his recent meetings with the Board. He gave a quick year-to-date summary of performance against key indicators.

Susan updated the team on her new development initiative focused on high-potential leaders, which spurred an animated discussion over who should participate.

And then it was Lauren's turn.

An athletic-looking redhead, she seemed comfortable and like a veteran of the team. She wore a slate-gray Torreys jacket from a collection they'd sold three seasons earlier, subtly letting everyone know that she'd had a connection to Torreys long before Brian hired her.

"I spent the last few months reviewing the sales data, interviewing our reps, and reading customer surveys," she said. "I ran focus groups and studied our competitors to see if we were missing anything, to see if there were gaps we could exploit.

"Torreys is riding high right now, and in my mind, that's the time to be bold and go after something new," Lauren said. "I know I'm new here, and I don't know all the history. That said, I'd still like us to consider introducing a new line that would appeal to teenagers and adults who don't have the same disposable income as current Torreys buyers."

We were impressed with Lauren's courage to challenge group assumptions. From our vantage point, we thought she did it in the right way: with a mix of confidence and humility.

Still, we were not surprised by the reaction. Faces around the table froze. Or fell. Peggy looked stricken. Susan dropped the pen out of her hand. And Victoria cut a look to Brian.

Susan was the first to regain composure and offer a response. "Look," she said, "I love the idea of being aggressive, but everyone in this room is maxed out right now. And it took us six months to find you. We can't staff up fast enough to take on anything that big."

Manny agreed with Susan and added that Torreys was a top-shelf brand name. In his opinion, going down-market would dilute the brand. "We're all as proud to wear our label as our customers are," he said. "We don't want to see our gear on the sales rack at some low-budget retailer."

Lauren tried to explain that a new line could stake out a whole new territory, go after a new and unexplored segment of the market. She tried to share examples from other companies, but other voices at the table were louder than hers. The opposing arguments seemed to pile one on top of another at an alarming rate. They flew so fast that it was hard to identify who was saying what.

"Torreys manufactures clothing in America, and that's impossible at a lower price point."

"Our customers love our designs. We can't offer the same detail at a lower price point."

"Our brand is that we are Made in America."

"This isn't who we are as a company."

"A second line would cannibalize our own success."

"It'd take away our cachet."

It sounded like the team was shutting down and refusing to have an honest conversation, which happens sometimes, even with Loyalist Teams. The people on these teams are not perfect, and they can respond in the moment, as all of us can, with fear and emotion. The best teams, however, can shake that off, reexamine themselves, and challenge their own invested orthodoxy or thinking. We knew Lauren had hit a chord because the resistance was so strong and so uniform across the team. She'd clearly stumbled onto something that needed to be challenged. And we were pleased to see her stay the course, even after the initial response.

Lauren sat silently through the immediate reactions, partly because she didn't see an opening to squeeze in a word, and partly because she hadn't expected such a torrent of nos.

When Peggy said, "Our brand promise is well-made, well-designed apparel for people to live in," Lauren could not sit tight any longer.

"What?" Lauren asked. "I'm not asking us to overthrow our brand promise or subvert our values. I just think if there's a way to pursue growth and expand our market, we should consider it. What am I missing here? Brian, is there a reason you're not saying much? You did tell me to bring this up, didn't you?"

Everyone looked to the CEO. And his face was hard to read. Then he glanced at us. We shook our heads to say we weren't bailing him out. "This is exactly the kind of conversation you all need to have, and you have the skills to do it," we said.

Brian agreed. "Look," he said, "Lauren, I hired you to bring new ideas, so yes, I want to have this conversation. And frankly, I don't know what I don't know. The last two years, I've been focused on Ops, then on the bake-off to get this job, then on managing the Board and hiring you to complete this team. I haven't yet focused on new opportunities for Torreys. And I want this whole team to be looking for ways to grow and improve our value proposition. That should be part of our DNA."

Everyone shifted in their seats as they processed and reacted to his comments.

Peggy leaned forward to explain her thought process. The last two years had been hectic for her too, and she'd survived the rough patches only by imaging that things would settle down so the team could fall into a steady routine.

"I thought we were just getting to that place," she said. "I thought we were in for some smooth sailing, so your idea caught me off guard and I overreacted.

"So," Peggy continued, "Let me start over. I'm sorry I jumped down your throat. That wasn't fair, and it's not how we treat each other. Lauren, this is a big idea, and I truly am curious to know more. I do want to hear about your research. What have you learned? What are the pros and cons? What other companies have you seen do this successfully?"

Lauren took a deep breath and thanked Peggy for her apology and her questions. She took the team through the rest of her research and waited.

Manny spoke first. "Wow," he said. "That is pretty compelling. I had no idea about the size of the opportunity."

Lauren responded to Manny and volleyed ideas back and forth with one team member at a time until everyone was in the thick of it. As people built off each other's ideas, the energy and pace of the conversation increased with the volume.

Victoria jumped up and grabbed a marker to capture what she could on the dry-erase board. "What do we need to know?" she asked.

"Where could we take cost out of production here in the US?" Brian asked.

"What if this were connected to a campaign to provide sports clothing to low-income schools?" Peggy asked.

"What are our non-negotiables? Would we ever off-shore under any circumstances?" Manny asked.

"Who should we benchmark?" Susan said. "And what other industries should we be looking at who have done this well?"

We were inspired by what we saw. One by one, people granted each other trust, suspended fears, and placed their personal or departmental agendas aside. The nervous, combative energy that started the conversation dissipated as the team began exploring the possibilities of this opportunity.

Within a couple hours, they'd drawn up lists of all they knew, all they needed to learn, and where they could find the necessary data. And at that point, they agreed to table the conversation for the day and circle back to it in a few weeks when each had completed their assignments.

Brian thanked the team for their efforts and said, "This was a tough one, maybe the toughest discussion we've had." He turned to us and added, "So, how'd we do?"

From our perspective, we thought they had done well, but it was important to know how the people engaged in the conversation had experienced it. As usual, we had questions for the team. We started with a few general queries:

How well did the conversation start?

What changed along the way?

Did everyone feel heard?

Did anyone feel railroaded at any point?

What were the pivot points for you?

Did you act like a Loyalist Team?

The responses were consistent. Everyone said they ultimately felt heard. Lauren said that early on, she wasn't sure. And she feared she had made a mistake.

"When everyone was saying no, it felt almost reactionary, like you guys were locked into some binary code where you could only say yes or no," she said. "And I knew it was too early to say yes and too early to say no. I thought this couldn't be the team I joined. Or the team that vetted me so hard. I thought I must have missed something."

Around her, people nodded. The veterans on the team realized they were the ones who had missed something. They'd temporarily forgotten that members of Loyalist Teams keep conversations open and remain curious. Members of these teams look for ways to support each other, and they know that winning isn't a zero-sum game.

Progress is rarely a yes/no proposition. And winning and losing don't divide the executive team. The people on the team only do either together.

Lauren's bold suggestion triggered intense emotions around the table. In their own ways, all the people at the table struggled with the same thing—fear. They didn't know if adding another line was too big a risk, if it would demand too much from each of them, or if it would dilute their brand and challenge the company's values. They were afraid that they—individually or collectively—would fail. So they said no, at first.

Feeling that resistance, Lauren felt like throwing up her arms.

"I thought about saying, 'Fine, you win,'" she admitted, "but when I asked Brian to jump in, I started to feel better because he engaged with the idea. And then everyone else did. Peggy, when you apologized for not listening, it really turned things around."

And that is what separates Loyalist Teams from the rest. Members of the team can disagree. They can be passionate about their positions. And they can feel fear, anger, or frustration—or all three at once. But even in their discomfort, they stay engaged.

Loyalists don't step out. They don't shut down. They don't shut anyone else out of the debate. They commit to combining their strengths and finding the solution.

The Torreys team didn't reach a yes or no answer on Lauren's suggestion, but that wasn't what she was after. She wanted the green light to explore and to know that she had their support.

We asked the Torreys team if this conversation showed them anything new about themselves.

Victoria spoke up first. "I'm amazed at the level of candor. People really go out there and say what they think," she said. "I've deferred to Brian for so long because well, he's Brian. But I wonder if that's lazy. If I defer to him, I can sit back and watch. And I think I need to follow Lauren's lead and be willing to go out there.

"She just got here, and she had faith that this team would support her," Victoria added.

"Of course," Peggy said, "we might get pointed and the conversation might heat up, but we're not going to let you fail. That's our thing, isn't it?"

Around the table, everyone agreed. And Brian just smiled, saying everything without saying a word.

We'd known Brian for years at this point. We met him when he was the newly promoted Chief Operations Officer. At that time, he was reserved in meetings and held back like Victoria did in this one. Over the years, though, we had watched him strengthen his technical skills, increase his capacity to think strategically, and delve deeper into understanding how the best teams work. We'd watched him wrestle with big ideas and learn to pull his team into these wrestling matches.

And this was one of those moments. Brian had invited us because he wasn't sure about something. He wanted to know if it was possible to change the lineup of his team while keeping the same dynamic that had served Torreys so well.

We knew that this was possible. The personalities on a team will change. People will undoubtedly come and go. And each addition and subtraction will change the personality of the team. But the mechanism that makes the team work can exist indefinitely.

Loyalist Teams are remarkably, bankably consistent in some aspects. The personnel don't have to be, but the traits, characteristics, and behaviors that make one team a Loyalist Team will make the next iteration of that team a Loyalist Team, as well as any future iterations.

We told the Torreys execs what they already knew: Loyalist Teams are sustained one relationship at a time and built by putting the toughest issues on the table and sticking with the discussion when it gets tough. And the Torreys team was doing just that.

LOYALIST TEAMS ROCK THE BOAT

Loyalist Teams consistently deliver extraordinary results. They're the teams we remember all our lives. On these teams, we do our best and most creative work, blow through challenges, and exceed our own expectations.

You know you're on a Loyalist Team when:

- You trust your teammates implicitly; they have your back and you have theirs

- You always assume positive intent

- Team members talk to each other, not about each other

- Team members hold each other accountable: poor performance isn't tolerated

- The team supports you, even when you make mistakes

- You see intelligent risk-taking and innovation

- The team habitually confronts the brutal facts

- You're having fun

- You can be your authentic self and do your best work every day

Loyalist Teams create value because:

- Good enough is never enough for them

- Team members push each other to do their very best work

- They talk about conflict right away and don't let issues fester

- They put the company agenda first

- There is a high level of engagement and performance

- Innovation and creativity grow exponentially

If you lead a Loyalist Team . . .

1. **Don't let the team get complacent.**
   Sustaining success is your biggest challenge. Being a Loyalist Team is not a destination; it is a journey. Nothing around the team will stay static, so the team must evolve and grow. Keep asking: "How do we make sure we are getting better?" Keep challenging the team to talk about what's next.
2. **Learn to learn.**
   Remind your team that setbacks and failure are *how* you learn. Make it safe for the team to take risks and stretch. Encourage the team to listen to and learn from each other and those outside the team. Bring in new and different points of view. Challenge conventional thinking whenever possible.
3. **Spread the wealth—create capacity in other leaders.**
   Your team got to this place with effort, learning, and intentional focus. Congratulations!

It's now your job to help other leaders learn to do the same. Are you mentoring other leaders who could benefit from your experience? Are you building Loyalist leadership capacity on the team?

4. **Drive uncompromising candor.**
When the team is this good and the relationships are so close, there's a tendency to hold back. Remember that the relationships are strong enough to survive the tough conversations.

5. **Don't be a Loyalist bully.**
The goal is to have a Loyalist organization. Don't make other teams within your company the common enemy in order to pull your team together. Set an example for other teams and bring them along.

If you are a member of a Loyalist Team . . .

1. **Push your teammates to achieve.**
Don't look to your leader to solve problems or own the toughest issues. Continuously give feedback—positive and negative. Push yourself and your teammates to speak with candor and discuss the undiscussable. Don't get comfortable and complacent.

2. **Remain curious and committed to learning.**
Stay fresh. What other perspectives might be valuable for you to consider? What else might shore up your weakness and allow you to leverage your strengths? Has the team

become too insular? Be sure the team isn't
falling into the trap of groupthink or believing it has all the right answers.

3. **Own and explore mistakes.**
   Don't hide from your mistakes. Instead, own
   them. Find the learning when your teammates
   make mistakes. Contribute to an environment that is about confronting reality, learning from setbacks, and showing vulnerability.

If this is you, if yours is a Loyalist Team, you know
how hard you've worked—and you should be proud of
the achievement. Teams don't get here without digging in and making a sustained commitment. And no
team stays here without continuing to apply the same
rigor going forward. You'll continue to do the work—
to question assumptions, to challenge one another, and
to take direct feedback—and you'll continue to achieve
as only the highest-performing teams can. Congratulations, and keep it up. You're in a rare group of exceptional teams.

7   THE TRUTH ABOUT TEAMS

Teams work, or they fail to work. And often, the people on them can't give the reasons for either outcome.

When teams fail, they often dissolve into cliques riddled with blame or confusion. You see it everywhere: The offensive line blames the quarterback for a late throw; the quarterback points to the wide receiver, who bobbled the ball; and the receiver looks back to the linemen who let the opponent run free and interfere with the pass. Everyone sees fault and assigns blame from their own vantage point.

On any team, the players can rarely step outside themselves to see the big picture or identify the issues that need attention. Without a stat sheet or instant replay, the team attempts to fix everything or nothing, or makes choices by trial and error.

We created the Loyalist Team 3D to prevent this type of guesswork. Our 360-degree assessment lets us examine the team from all sides and measure a team's tendencies, traits, and characteristics. It also gave us a wide, landscape-like view of all teams across all the industries in which we work.

As we measured team after team, year after year, we collected the dimensions of each one and stored them in a database. Once we'd worked with enough teams to have a meaningful sample size, we analyzed the data and looked for patterns. We parsed the mountains of detail and read the message hidden there. And the message was clear.

RELATIONSHIPS MATTER

The difference between Saboteur, Benign Saboteur, Situational Loyalist, and Loyalist Teams depends on several factors, but relationships reign supreme. Relationships among team members account for 70 percent of the variance between team types.

If you want to predict how effective a team is, look at the relationships on that team. The quality of relationships is the number one predictor of whether a team is a high-performing Loyalist Team, a value-destroying Saboteur Team, or something in the middle.

Extraordinary teams are built on extraordinary relationships. Hiring extraordinary individuals and cultivating brilliant ideas can go a long way, but to boost the power of either, the data gives clear direction: work on strengthening the relationships. In predicting team effectiveness, relationships matter more than the strength of the leader, the actions a team takes collectively, and the mindset that team members bring to the job.

On the best teams, our database shows, the team leader creates an environment of excellence, and every member of the team supports and sustains that environment by reinforcing the standards of excellence.

In other words, no one is off the hook. No one can phone it in or neglect his or her responsibilities as a teammate—not if he or she wants to be part of a Loyalist Team and reap the rewards. It doesn't matter if you are the team leader, a team veteran, or the newest member of the team. If you want to move your team forward, work to strengthen the relationships you have with your teammates.

Loyalist Teams are made of Loyalist relationships. It may sound ridiculously obvious, but think about it the other way: you cannot build a Loyalist Team if you're not willing to build Loyalist relationships. These are the one-to-one connections in which each person assumes the other has positive intent and extends trust. It's a reciprocal relationship in which each person shares information and lends a hand when necessary. Both people put the team's agenda first. Both people talk about challenges as they arise. And both people commit to each other's success.

Every member of the team has to play if your team wants to be a Loyalist Team. That is why creating a Loyalist Team is a team sport: even the leader cannot control every relationship. And each person can only control one side of any relationship. When working with clients, we often suggest that each person start by examining and owning his or her own behaviors.

This is a good place for you to start. Whatever your formal role on your team, review the relationships you have with your teammates and focus on the ones that need repair. This is the biggest lever you have to move your team along the continuum of effectiveness.

If you're on a Saboteur Team, identify the Saboteur relationships that you are a part of and consider how to make them better. Ask yourself if you are assuming positive intent, extending trust, and sharing information. If the answer to any of those is no, then you're the Saboteur in the relationship. And you can change that.

If yours is a Situational Loyalist Team, identify the relationships that are spotty or the situations in which you fail to get someone's back. And you can make those relationships more consistent and more Loyalist in nature.

Change isn't easy. We know that. And if "work to strengthen your relationships" feels too general, we drilled deeper into the data to identify the specific practices that the best teams use to keep their relationships in shape. If you're not on a Loyalist Team, you can follow their lead.

MAKE A SET OF OPERATING NORMS AND LIVE BY THEM

Loyalist Teams are seventy-three times more likely than Saboteur Teams to have a set of norms that spell out the rules of the road. You can work with your team to create a unique set that reflects the culture you wish to have, the industry in which you work, and the goals you hope to achieve.

Each of the teams in Chapters 3–6 created sets of operating norms that you can look to for guidance in creating yours. Often these lists include statements like:

I will proactively share information.

I will ask questions instead of making assumptions.

I will talk to you, not about you.

I will hold myself accountable to the team's high standards.

I will take responsibility to ensure that my concerns are heard.

Once you and your team have created and agreed upon a set of norms, you have to take one more step if you want to really leverage the power of teamwork. You have to put teeth into the norms. Individuals must be prepared to call out team members who fail to play by the rules they've agreed to, and there must be consequences when someone breaks or bends the rules.

Loyalist Teams are 125 times more likely than Saboteur Teams to address unacceptable behaviors promptly. And they are seven times more likely to address them than Situational Loyalist Teams.

More than that, on Loyalist Teams, members don't wait for the boss. Of all four team types, Loyalist Teams are the only ones in which team members consistently hold each other accountable without an overreliance on the team leader.

EXTEND TRUST

Putting faith in another person can be a tricky thing, so it's important to understand what trust means among members of a team. On high-performance teams, individuals trust each other's intent. On the leadership team at Torreys, for example, two members of the team were competing for one job—and not just any job. Brian and Helen were competing for the top job.

But even with the chief executive title hanging in the balance, the two candidates and all their teammates were able to remain a Loyalist Team because everyone trusted that everyone else had the same goal: the company's sustained success.

When Brian presented to Torreys' Board of Directors, Helen knew his actions could edge her out of the job, but she trusted that his motivating force had nothing to do with her. He was striving to improve the company's performance, the same as she was. When Helen led her team to double-digit sales growth, Brian knew he would benefit from her efforts even if he remained COO and she was selected as the new CEO.

Through the years and through the transition, the executives at Torreys worked continuously to build and maintain trust. When we reviewed the data from all the teams we've studied, we saw that Torreys was not alone. *Loyalist Teams are forty-seven times more likely* than Saboteur Teams to work hard to build and maintain trust. They are thirteen times more likely than even the Situational Loyalists to work on trust.

The data also showed exactly why trust matters: *Loyalist Teams are 292 times more likely* than Saboteur Teams to spend time debating, discussing problems, and making decisions.

Teams that trust each other enough to freely debate ideas and openly discuss problems are infinitely more likely to come to a solution that works and make a decision that sticks. On a Saboteur Team, like the Los Angeles office of North Star Financial under Matt's leadership, people close their doors and don't mention it even if they see the business going sideways. And when individuals are struggling, they don't say a word or ask for help.

On an individual level, trust gives people the space and safety to ask for help. *On Loyalist Teams, individuals are twenty-six times more likely* to feel comfortable asking for help than members of Saboteur Teams. And they are twice as likely to ask for help as their counterparts on Situational Loyalist Teams.

LEARN TO HAVE THE TOUGH CONVERSATIONS

Even on the best teams, individuals disagree. And disagreements can become heated. Individuals care passionately about their work, and occasionally the different visions for the future collide. Conflict is inevitable. But the highest-performing teams know how to work through it. The lesser teams don't.

Saboteur Teams are forty times more likely than Loyalist Teams to have a list of "undiscussables." These can be ideas, events, or even people who must not be named. Benign Saboteur Teams also routinely avoid the hard topics.

At G Street Technologies, for example, when the two teams first came together, no one could say what everyone knew: that the two former rivals had not morphed into one cohesive team even twelve months after the merger. Everyone from MassTech respected their new G Street colleagues. And all the original G Streeters thought the talent acquired from MassTech was brilliant. Yet no one from either company could say, "We are operating in silos, and we need to tear them down."

As long as they operated in these dual cones of silence, the smartest computational biologists on the planet could not get anything done. They missed deadlines and started losing market share until finally, after two days of hard work at an off-site location, they learned to place the thorny issues on the table and talk about them.

Soon after the full team learned to talk about how they were divided, they learned how to solve the problem. They were able to suture up those divisions and get back to business. It took some time and was not always comfortable—or as Jane said, "It wasn't all rainbows and unicorns"—but they moved up to a Situational Loyalist designation. And later, the team took the last bold step toward high performance.

Once G Streeters learned to reach across the team and discuss the previously undiscussable topics, they learned to be more direct and to give each other feedback. These conversations are rarely easy. Loyalist Teams do it anyway. *Members of Loyalist Teams are 103 times more likely* than members of Saboteur Teams to challenge one another to achieve high standards of performance. They are 106 times more likely to give direct feedback.

LEADERSHIP MATTERS TOO

Relationships play the biggest role in dividing teams among the four team types. But the team leader contributes too. After you consider the impact of relationships, leadership is the most meaningful variance between Saboteur, Benign Saboteur, Situational Loyalist, and Loyalist Teams.

The leader sets standards that everyone understands, roots out destructive behaviors, and demonstrates a personal commitment to the team.

The most effective leaders go further. They create a supportive climate that encourages everyone to take risks and learn from their mistakes. The leader who creates this type of climate is 111 times more likely to be on a Loyalist Team than on a Saboteur Team. She's also more likely to make sure every team member has a clear understanding of the team's purpose or vision.

On ATR's North American Sales Team, for example, Kathryn assembled a team of skilled and driven professionals. She showed her personal commitment to them one team member at a time by making herself endlessly available to discuss issues and remove obstacles from their paths. Still, her team sat stuck in second gear, grinding away as a Situational Loyalist Team when there was no shortage of talent or ambition. None of the ATR Sales leaders wanted to settle for good when great was available. Every one of them wanted to be a Loyalist Team.

They made the leap when Kathryn convened the troops and made sure that everyone understood what they needed to do together and what they could only achieve together. She instructed them to talk to each other, share best practices, and troubleshoot with each other before coming to her. When we met with Kathryn and her team six months after our initial meeting, we asked them to complete the Loyalist Team 3D a second time, and they landed squarely in the Loyalist Team designation.

We saw their improvement in the assessment scores, and we know others saw it too.

STAKEHOLDERS SEE MORE THAN YOU THINK

Teams often think they're like Las Vegas: what happens in the team stays in the team.

The truth is much more transparent.

Stakeholders include the team's internal clients and the team's direct reports. They can include members of the communications department who have to share news with investors, and they can include members of the compliance department who have to work with regulators. All of these people care about the team's effectiveness, and the team cannot hide from any of them.

When stakeholders are asked to evaluate a team, *Loyalist Teams are forty-six times more likely* to be judged effective than Situational Loyalist Teams by the team's stakeholders. And when compared to Saboteur Teams, they're not in the same ballpark, the same area code, or the same universe.

Loyalist Teams are two thousand times more likely to be rated as effective than Saboteur Teams. Yes, two thousand.

Compared to Saboteur Teams, Loyalist Teams are:

292 times more likely to spend time debating, discussing problems, and making decisions

111 times more likely to have a leader who creates an atmosphere of intelligent risk-taking and encourages members to learn from mistakes

106 times more likely to give each other tough feedback, even if it's hard to hear

55 times more likely to have very well-defined goals for the team

47 times more likely to work hard to build and maintain trust

35 times more likely to demonstrate that they are committed to each other's success

26 times more likely to feel comfortable asking for help from each other when they are struggling or uncertain

MAINTAINING A LOYALIST TEAM

Loyalist Teams consistently deliver extraordinary work because members of these teams consistently work on being Loyalists to one another.

As we said in the beginning of this book, Loyalist Teams have identifiable and replicable traits and characteristics. Individuals on these teams—leaders and members alike—learn the behaviors and commit to practicing them. They know that occasionally, they will make mistakes, let each other down, and fall short of their goals. None of us is perfect. But members of these teams always know how to get back on track.

If you want to maintain a Loyalist Team . . .

1. **Trust your teammates unconditionally.**
   Team members extend trust to one another without demanding that anyone prove their loyalty. They trust each other through the good times and the bad.
2. **Assume positive intent, or ask questions until you can.**
   Team members give each other the benefit of the doubt. They check their own judgments or set aside any stories they may have heard about each other's motivations or intent. If a member of a Loyalist Team can't understand another member's behavior, they talk with that person directly instead of making assumptions or grousing to someone else.
3. **Talk to your teammates, not about them.**
   Team members discuss challenges directly. They don't engage in gossip and instead choose to work out differences in a respectful and timely manner. Every member demonstrates loyalty to all the other team members.
4. **Care about your teammates' success as you care about your own.**
   Team members take the time to help and support each other. They step in when there is a problem or challenge that someone can't solve on his own. Each person makes personal

sacrifices to help others and gives candid guidance to help a teammate learn and grow.

5. **Put the team's agenda ahead of your own.**
   Team members sacrifice resources and personal recognition to ensure the team can reach the most important goals. Everyone keeps her ego in check and focuses on a broader view of goals so the whole team can see how each part fits into the greater whole.

6. **Push your teammates to do their best work. And expect them to push you to do yours.**
   Team members challenge each other to reach shared goals. No one wants to let a teammate down, so they work harder and try more. Loyalists don't spend energy watching their own backs, so they can take risks and reach higher.

7. **Discuss the toughest issues in the room with members of your team and leave the room fully aligned.**
   Team members engage in rigorous debate. They discuss the toughest business and team issues by voicing and debating conflicting opinions. They reach an agreement and stick to it.

8. **Give your teammates feedback, even when it's hard.**
   Team members give direct feedback to each other. Everyone agrees to tell each other the tough messages so that everyone can correct mistakes and improve his or her performance.

8 HOW TO MAKE YOUR TEAM GREAT

By now, it's no secret that we are wildly passionate about the extraordinary power of great teams. And after decades of being *on* teams, *leading* teams, *consulting with* teams, and ultimately *studying* every last detail of them—from the best teams that create unimaginable results to the miserable and dysfunctional teams that destroy value with every touch—we can say with complete certainty that Loyalist Teams inspire people to give, and to be, their very best.

So our question for you is, why settle for anything less?

If you work on a team—and nearly all of us do—why not work on a Loyalist Team? Given the many hours we spend at work each week, why not make it the best experience it can be?

All too often, we see teams that settle for less for a number of reasons.

Another reason is faulty logic. Periodically, we meet leaders who've studied teamwork, drawn the wrong conclusions, and fostered a cutthroat culture in which everyone is out for themselves. These leaders erroneously believe that a mindset of "If I win, you lose" will bring out the best in people. They believe it will motivate high performance. It won't. This mindset may benefit one person while discouraging many and failing the organization at large.

While we know that Loyalist Teams are made up of highly competitive members, these individuals use their competitive drive to pull their teammates up to the highest standard. They join forces to defeat the real competition that sits outside their company.

We've worked with a few leaders who have said, "I like to keep my team members off-balance and at odds with each other. Sometimes I stoke the flames of jealousy to keep them sharp and competing with each other."

Competition may keep the team members throwing sharp elbows at one another, but it won't force the team to achieve anything together. The best teams improve team performance because team members don't let each other fail and they hold themselves accountable for the entire team's performance.

Another common reason that teams muddle along is that the team leaders undervalue the impact of building a Loyalist Team. Because they undervalue the outcome, they seriously underinvest in the necessary input. Many teams spend little or even no time on developing relationships within the team and making the serious and ongoing effort it takes to build and maintain a Loyalist Team. They spend time discussing business strategy, and they may schedule team dinners or golf outings, but they dedicate zero time to focusing on the team itself. The results are predictable: unresolved conflict, misaligned goals, and unclear expectations. At best, these teams maintain their passivity (Benign Saboteurs) or descend into Saboteur hell.

Another reason we often see teams languish is that the process of building a great team feels overwhelming and mystifying. Team leaders can see the dysfunction and want to fix it, but they simply don't know where to start. And with so many other business challenges and the volume of work most of us face, team development gets pushed to the side to deal with at a later date.

Team members on underperforming teams often don't realize they have a choice. They assume the difference between an awesome team and a disappointing one is a matter of luck. If they're on the losing end, they hope to outlast this bad team experience—maybe the scary boss will get promoted or the jerk of a teammate will get fired. However it happens, they hope that this too shall pass.

But everyone has a choice.

We were compelled to write this book because we want you to be able to exercise that choice. We believe that everyone deserves a great team experience, today and every day. We wanted to give that experience a name and explain the logic behind great teams. We wanted to break down its component parts so that you could decide to make the effort and know exactly what steps to get to the finish line.

We didn't want you to have to reach back to a high school sports team to relive your best team experience. And we know that even lesser teams can pull together in a moment of crisis, but we didn't want you to have to rely on some traumatic event to understand the power and the pleasure of serving on a high-performing team.

In our work, we serve on several teams. The four of us who started Trispective are one team. And whenever any one of us works with a client's team, we join that team too. We teach them the traits and characteristics of a Loyalist Team and show them the steps necessary to get there. Our clients return the favor. They show us how the model can be applied to different teams in different industries. They also teach us different ways to explain, implement, and interpret the lessons of great teamwork. Many of our clients inspire us with their actions and with their words.

All of our clients will tell you the same thing. Building and maintaining a Loyalist Team is not easy. The actions that a Loyalist Team demands from its members are not without risk or serious investment of time and energy. And there can be no shortage of courage.

So, if you're hesitant to do the hard work, we understand. And if you're wondering whether you want to make the commitment to build a Loyalist Team, we hear you. But consider this: Saboteur Teams are hard work too. On them, people expend tremendous amounts of energy watching their backs, protecting or hoarding resources, sleuthing out the unspoken rules, and strategizing how to navigate the politics around them.

Staying afloat on a Benign Saboteur Team may require less active energy, but it's lonely and uninspiring. The results are underwhelming. Even with Situational Loyalist Teams, where there are pockets of strong relationship and trust, you're not leveraging all the strengths and talents on the team.

Teamwork, in general, can be messy and uncomfortable and difficult to get right because teams are made up of individuals who arrive on the scene with their own beliefs, fears, philosophies, and habits that may or may not work within the group.

But so what?

Are you going to use that as an excuse to settle for a team that doesn't make you happy or help you reach your goals?

Our passion, and our unwavering goal, is to see you and your team thrive. So we'll ask you again: Why settle for anything less?

You have all the tools you need. Now go out and build the team of your dreams.

ACKNOWLEDGMENTS

To our husbands, Bill, Nikk, Scott, and Tim. Without your constant love and support, the fulfilling careers we have enjoyed, the work of Trispective, and this book would not have been possible.

To our children, Adam, Alex, Althea, Annalise, Archie, Drew, Iain, Josh, Nathan, Sam, and Seri, and our families, thanks for being the loudest voices in our cheering section.

To Barb Pomeroy, thank you for your steadfast commitment, support, and friendship. You make a difference every day. To Scott Baker, we are grateful for your research, brainpower, and expertise that helped shape the Loyalist Team model. And to our Trispective team, thank you for living the Loyalist principles every day. To Jody, thank you for your incredible ability to translate our stories and years of collective wisdom into the written word in a most compelling way. We are so grateful to be touched by your gift.

To Mel Parker and Colleen Lawrie, thanks for your belief in us, for your guidance, and for pushing us to be better than we thought we could be. To Melissa Veronesi and Beth Partin, thank you for making us look smart by making our copy clean.

To our many friends along the way, thank you for being a special part of our personal journeys. You have made the trip worthwhile, and we are grateful. To the leaders we have worked for and worked with throughout our careers, we appreciate how you have shown us what it takes to create incredible teams and organizations. You've inspired us. We are better leaders, consultants, and business pioneers as a result of you.

To our clients, you are this book. You give us a sense of purpose every day.

Finally, to all who take the time to read this book, we wrote this for you because everyone deserves a great team.

LINDA ADAMS, ABBY CURNOW-CHAVEZ, AUDREY EPSTEIN, AND REBECCA TEASDALE honed their expertise inside some of the largest and most powerful businesses operating today. The four authors have led the human resources, talent management, leadership development, and organizational effectiveness functions of multiple Fortune 500 companies like Ford Motor Company, PepsiCo, Newmont Mining, Accenture, and Level 3 Communications. Currently, the four comprise The Trispective Group, catering to companies like PetSmart, Equinix, Kaiser Permanente, Hitachi Data Systems, Vail Resorts, and others.

PublicAffairs is a publishing house founded in 1997. It is a tribute to the standards, values, and flair of three persons who have served as mentors to countless reporters, writers, editors, and book people of all kinds, including me.

I. F. Stone, proprietor of *I. F. Stone's Weekly*, combined a commitment to the First Amendment with entrepreneurial zeal and reporting skill and became one of the great independent journalists in American history. At the age of eighty, Izzy published *The Trial of Socrates*, which was a national bestseller. He wrote the book after he taught himself ancient Greek.

Benjamin C. Bradlee was for nearly thirty years the charismatic editorial leader of *The Washington Post*. It was Ben who gave the *Post* the range and courage to pursue such historic issues as Watergate. He supported his reporters with a tenacity that made them fearless and it is no accident that so many became authors of influential, best-selling books.

Robert L. Bernstein, the chief executive of Random House for more than a quarter century, guided one of the nation's premier publishing houses. Bob was personally responsible for many books of political dissent and argument that challenged tyranny around the globe. He is also the founder and longtime chair of Human Rights Watch, one of the most respected human rights organizations in the world.

· · ·

For fifty years, the banner of Public Affairs Press was carried by its owner Morris B. Schnapper, who published Gandhi, Nasser, Toynbee, Truman, and about 1,500 other authors. In 1983, Schnapper was described by *The Washington Post* as "a redoubtable gadfly." His legacy will endure in the books to come.

Peter Osnos, *Founder and Editor-at-Large*